YORK NOTES

TO KILL A MOCKINGBIRD

HARPER LEE

NOTES BY BETH SIMS

Longman
is an imprint of

PEARSON

York Press

YORK PRESS
322 Old Brompton Road, London SW5 9JH

PEARSON EDUCATION LIMITED
Edinburgh Gate, Harlow,
Essex CM20 2JE, United Kingdom
Associated companies, branches and representatives throughout the world

First published 1997
New edition 2002
This new and fully revised edition 2010

10 9 8 7 6 5 4 3 2 1

ISBN 978–1–4082–4883–6

Illustrated by Gay Galsworthy; and Neil Gower (p. 6 only)
Photograph of Harper Lee used by kind permission of Corbis Images

Phototypeset by Border Consultants, Dorset

Printed in the UK

CONTENTS

PART FOUR
KEY CONTEXTS AND THEMES

PART FIVE
LANGUAGE AND STRUCTURE

PART SIX
GRADE BOOSTER

PART ONE: INTRODUCTION

Study and revision advice

There are TWO main stages to your reading and work on *To Kill a Mockingbird*. Firstly, the study of the book as you read it. Secondly, your preparation or revision for the exam or controlled assessment. These top tips will help you with both.

 READING AND STUDYING THE NOVEL – DEVELOP INDEPENDENCE!

- Try to engage and respond **personally** to the characters, ideas and story – not just for your enjoyment, but also because it helps you develop your own **independent ideas and thoughts** about *To Kill a Mockingbird*. This is something that examiners are very keen to see.

- **Talk** about the text with friends and family; ask questions in class; put forward your own viewpoint – and, if time, **read around** the text to find out about life in the 1930s during the Great Depression in the American South.

- Take time to **consider** and **reflect** on the **key elements** of the novel; keep your own notes, mind-maps, diagrams, scribbled jottings about the characters and how you respond to them; follow the story as it progresses [what do you think might happen?]; discuss the main themes and ideas [what do *you* think it is about? Prejudice? Growing up? Courage?]; pick out language that impresses you or makes an **impact**, and so on.

- Treat your studying **creatively**. When you write essays or give talks about the book make your responses creative. Think about using really clear ways of explaining yourself, use unusual quotations, well-chosen vocabulary, and try powerful, persuasive ways of beginning or ending what you say or write.

 REVISION – DEVELOP ROUTINES AND PLANS!

- **Good revision** comes from **good planning**. Find out when your exam or controlled assessment is and then plan to look at key aspects of *To Kill a Mockingbird* on different days or times during your revision period. You could use these Notes – see **How can these Notes help me?** – and add dates or times when you are going to cover a particular topic.

- Use **different ways** of **revising**. Sometimes talking about the text and what you know/don't know with a friend or member of the family can help; other times, filling a sheet of A4 with all your ideas in different colour pens about a character, for example Atticus, can make ideas come alive; other times, making short lists of quotations to learn, or numbering events in the plot, can assist you.

- **Practise plans** and **essays**. As you get nearer the 'day', start by looking at essay **questions** and writing short bulleted plans. Do several plans [you don't have to write the whole essay]; then take those plans and add details to them [quotations, linked ideas]. Finally, using the advice in **Part Six: Grade Booster**, write some practice essays and then check them out against the advice we have provided.

> **EXAMINER'S TIP**
>
> Prepare for the exam/controlled assessment! Whatever you need to bring, make sure you have it with you – books, if you're allowed, pens, pencils – and that you turn up on time!

Introducing *To Kill a Mockingbird*

SETTING AND LOCATION

To Kill a Mockingbird is set in 1933–5 in Maycomb, a small, fictitious town based on Harper Lee's home town Monroeville, Alabama, in the American South. It is a time and place dominated by economic depression, racial segregation and prejudice against African-Americans.

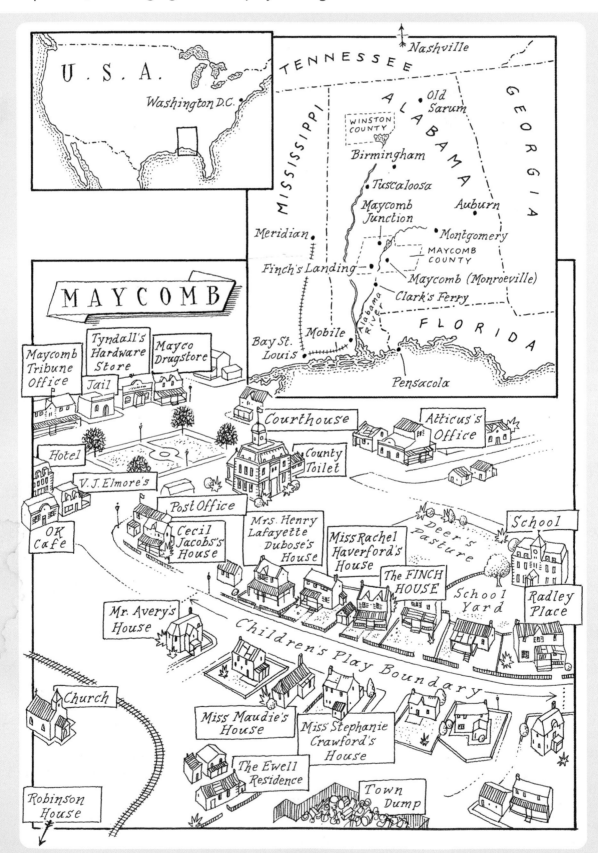

CHARACTERS: WHO'S WHO

Scout

Jem

Atticus

Dill

Calpurnia

Boo Radley

Miss Maudie Atkinson

Tom Robinson

Aunt Alexandra

HARPER LEE: AUTHOR AND CONTEXT

1926 Nelle Harper Lee is born in Monroeville, Alabama.

1929 Following the Wall Street Crash, the Great Economic Depression causes widespread poverty and unemployment.

1931 The Scottsboro incident occurs; nine black young men are falsely charged and found guilty of raping two white women in Alabama.

1933 President Roosevelt introduces policies to alleviate the effects of the Depression.

1945–9 Harper Lee starts (but never completes) a law degree at the State University of Alabama.

1950s Harper Lee gives up work as an airline reservations clerk in New York to write full-time, fine-tuning her novel over many years.

1954 The Civil Rights Movement, with Martin Luther King as an important leader, begins in Montgomery, Alabama.

1960 *To Kill a Mockingbird* is published and is an immediate bestseller.

1962 After winning the Pulitzer Prize and several other literary awards, the novel is made into a film.

Present Harper Lee divides her time between New York City and Monroeville, keeping out of the public eye.

PART TWO: PLOT AND ACTION

Plot summary: what happens in *To Kill a Mockingbird*?

REVISION ACTIVITY

- Go through the summaries for Parts One and Two below and **highlight** what you think are the **key moments**.

- Then find each moment in the **text** and **reread** it. Write down **two reasons** why you think each moment is so **important**.

PART ONE

- Jean Louise Finch (nicknamed Scout) starts school in September 1933, the story having commenced in early summer 1933.

- Scout can already read and write and her teacher, Miss Caroline Fisher, does not approve.

- We meet Walter Cunningham, the son of one of the families featured later in the novel. He is poor and has no lunch.

- Jem, Scout's brother, invites Walter home for lunch and Scout is openly appalled at his table manners. Calpurnia, the Finches' housekeeper, scolds Scout.

- Burris Ewell, one of Scout's classmates from a family we will meet again later, has headlice and upsets his teacher by using bad language. She is comforted by her students.

- In the spring and summer of 1933 and 1934 Jem, Scout and Dill, their friend, are fascinated by Boo Radley, their mysterious neighbour who has not been seen by the public for many years.

- Jem and Scout find presents in a knot-hole of an oak tree beside the Radley Place.

- The children invent a drama in which they play characters based on the Radley household.

- The children are focused on how to communicate with Boo Radley and make him come out of his house.

- One evening the children are frightened by a shadow and rush to escape. In the commotion Jem's trousers are torn off and he later finds them folded and mended on the fence.

- Jem and Scout find more presents and Jem begins to suspect that Boo has left them for the children.

- Mr Nathan Radley, Boo's keeper, fills up the knot-hole.

- After Atticus has shot a mad dog in the street, Jem and Scout pass Mrs Dubose's house and do not enjoy the verbal attacks from her.

- In anger one day, after Mrs Dubose has shouted vicious things about their father Atticus standing up for black people in his forthcoming law case, Jem knocks the heads off her camellia bushes.

- As a punishment enforced by Atticus, Jem is made to read to Mrs Dubose every night for a month.

- Before Mrs Dubose's death she leaves a single white camellia for Jem.
- Scout and Jem learn from Atticus that Mrs Dubose had been cantankerous as she had been courageously fighting a morphine addiction and had been determined to rid herself of the addiction before she died.

PART TWO

- Jem and Scout accompany Calpurnia to the black people's church and Aunt Alexandra comes to stay.
- Heck Tate, the town sheriff, tells Atticus they are moving Tom Robinson, a black man soon to be on trial, to the local jail and warns of trouble from a lynch mob.
- Jem and Scout notice Atticus disapear. They follow him.
- They find Atticus outside the Maycomb jail, guarding Tom Robinson, and a gang gathers around him.
- Jem, Scout and Dill sense trouble and come to try to help Atticus, who tells them to go home. Jem refuses.
- Following Scout's innocent friendliness, Mr Cunningham disperses the crowd of men.

- In summer 1935 the trial commences – Tom Robinson is accused of rape by Mayella Ewell, a poor white girl.
- Atticus, a lawyer, establishes that Mayella's bruises were the result of blows dealt by a strong left hand. Robert Ewell, Mayella's father, agrees that Mayella's right eye was bruised.
- Atticus reveals to the court that Robert Ewell is ambidextrous.

- As Tom has no use of his left hand, Atticus demonstrates that it couldn't have been Tom who dealt the blows.
- Tom is shown to be polite and honest, in contrast to Mayella and Robert Ewell.
- Jem believes the case is won, but Scout is not so sure.
- Jem and Scout are surprised that the white jury finds Tom Robinson guilty.
- Robert Ewell seeks revenge upon Atticus for the Ewells' humiliation in court.
- Atticus interrupts the Missionary Society tea with the news that Tom Robinson has been killed when trying to escape, and asks Calpurnia to accompany him to tell Tom's wife, Helen.

- As Scout and Jem return from a Halloween pageant, Robert Ewell attacks them with a knife.
- Boo Radley comes to the children's rescue. Jem is injured and carried back unconscious to the Finch home by Boo.
- Robert Ewell is found dead on top of his knife.
- The sheriff persuades Atticus to keep details of the incident quiet to protect Boo from trouble, highlighting the important message: 'it's a sin to kill a mockingbird' (Chapter 10, p. 96).
- Scout finally gets to see Boo and says 'he was real nice'. Atticus replies, rounding off the story with the message that he has reiterated throughout: 'Most people are, Scout, when you finally see them' (Chapter 31, p. 287).

PART ONE

Chapter 1: When it all began

SUMMARY

❶ The history of the Finch family, the town of Maycomb and the Radleys (the Finches' neighbours) is described, and the main characters, Scout, Jem, Atticus and Calpurnia, are introduced.

❷ Jem is almost ten and Scout nearly six when they meet Dill, who is nearly seven. Dill comes every summer from Mississippi to stay with Miss Rachel Haverford, his aunt and the Finches' neighbour.

❸ Jem, Scout and Dill become fascinated with the Radleys, who are rarely seen. Boo Radley has not left his house in fifteen years, ever since he got into trouble with other teenage boys and later supposedly attacked his father with a pair of scissors.

❹ The children are surprised when Calpurnia speaks badly of Mr Radley as she doesn't usually comment on white people's behaviour.

❺ Dill dares Jem to knock on the Radleys' door. Nothing happens, but they think they see an inside shutter move.

WHY IS THIS CHAPTER IMPORTANT?

A We are introduced to the narrative voice and perspective that will be used throughout.

B Harper Lee gives us information that helps us understand how important family background and family characteristics are in this society, and this will become significant for later events.

C We are introduced to the theme of growing up and childhood games – an important topic in the first part of the novel.

D The Maycomb setting is established. It is described on p. 11 as a **character**, 'old' and 'tired', but also with hope (it was a time of 'vague optimism').

E The chapter reveals the small-town mentality and the divisions and prejudices that exist in Maycomb, where there are different rules for black people and white people.

NARRATIVE VOICE AND PERSPECTIVE

Jean Louise Finch (nicknamed Scout as a child) is the **first-person narrator** as well as a participant in the story. Events are recounted first-hand, through a child's eyes. However, Scout is also describing events in retrospect; we see the story evolve not only from a child's viewpoint but also from a mature, adult perspective, offering the benefit of hindsight. The two different viewpoints are years apart.

The insightful narration by the adult Scout contrasts with the point of view, wit and humour expressed by the child Scout. As the novel deals with the main character growing up, it is a **bildungsroman**.

The two perspectives give the story's events some objectivity. However, even the narrator admits that this has its limitations, and that different people will always have different perspectives on events (a key message of the novel).

THE THEME OF RACIAL PREJUDICE

Although it is later in the novel that this main **theme** is fully established, useful background is introduced here. We are reminded of the recent history of black slavery in Alabama, USA, when we learn that Simon Finch, a family ancestor, bought three slaves.

Calpurnia's comment on Mr Radley, that he was 'the meanest man ever God blew breath into' (Chapter 1, p. 18), and the children's surprise at her saying something, is significant. As African-Americans at this time had a lower status in society, it would have been considered very out of place, even disrespectful, for them to comment on the ways of a white person.

This is echoed much later in the book, when Tom Robinson makes a major mistake in court by telling the white jury that he felt sorry for Mayella Ewell, a white girl.

EXAMINER'S TIP: WRITING ABOUT THE FINCH FAMILY BACKGROUND

It is important to consider characters in a rounded way by looking at what an author tells us about their history.

We learn that the Finch family was established over a hundred years ago, and that Atticus left Finch's Landing, the family homestead, to study in Montgomery before moving to Maycomb to practise law. Therefore, Atticus and his brother, who also left to study medicine, showed initiative and enterprise. In contrast, Aunt Alexandra stayed at Finch's Landing.

We discover that Atticus's wife died when Scout was two and that Atticus has to do the job of both parents – 'he played with us, read to us, and treated us with courteous detachment' (p. 11).

Calpurnia, the African-American housekeeper, has helped to take care of the children since Atticus's wife's death and often seems to take on the role of disciplinarian, which Scout sometimes resents as Atticus always takes Calpurnia's side (p. 12).

We see that just as Atticus is an individual breaking away from family tradition by setting himself up as a lawyer and leaving the Landing, he also believes in treating his African-American housekeeper with respect and his children as individuals.

KEY CONNECTIONS

Black Like Me (1960) is a true story told by John Howard Griffin, who disguises himself as a black man to experience what this is like in the American South in the late 1950s.

KEY QUOTE

Scout (narrator): 'I maintain that the Ewells started it all, but Jem, who was four years my senior, said it started long before that' (p. 9).

Chapters 2–3: An education begins?

SUMMARY

❶ Dill goes home and Scout and Jem begin school, Scout for the first time.

❷ Scout's teacher discovers Scout is literate and scolds her.

❸ Walter Cunningham refuses to borrow money. Scout tries to explain his behaviour and is punished.

❹ Scout starts a fight with Walter. Jem intervenes and invites Walter home for lunch.

❺ Calpurnia scolds Scout for commenting on Walter's table manners.

❻ Miss Caroline is frightened by Burris Ewell's jumping 'cootie' (Chapter 3, p. 31), and pupils try to explain to her about the Ewell family.

❼ Atticus encourages Scout to look at her school experiences in a new light.

WHY ARE THESE CHAPTERS IMPORTANT?

A The author **satirises** education, inviting the reader to consider its purpose.

B The Maycomb community and family characteristics are described in more detail.

C Scout learns that other figures of authority are not like Atticus, and her world view – previously confined to her house and street – expands a little.

D Scout and Jem's relationship is further explored.

E The child's viewpoint increases the story's impact. While Scout is puzzled by Miss Caroline's actions and reactions, the reader can understand why certain events are occurring. This perspective brings humour into the story.

CHECKPOINT 1

Is the hairlouse incident an effective way to introduce the Ewell family? Why?

EXAMINER'S TIP

Flashbacks to past events are often used by the author, for instance when Scout tells us that she learnt of the Cunninghams from a conversation she overheard last year. This makes the story **realistic**, as a past and a future are implied as well as a present. The novel is in fact one large flashback.

KNOWLEDGE OF THE MAYCOMB COMMUNITY

The families in this society are so distinct, with universally acknowledged characteristics, that Scout presumes her teacher should know them: 'Miss Caroline, he's a Cunningham' (Chapter 2, p. 26).

By making Miss Caroline a naive outsider, the author has an opportunity to acquaint the reader with Maycomb's inhabitants. We need to be informed about the Ewell and Cunningham families for later events. We see how close-knit the Maycomb community is when the children are able to stereotype and make generalisations about particular groups of people that Miss Caroline, from North Alabama, cannot understand.

We also see how deep-set many presumptions and prejudices are in this community. Miss Caroline is treated with suspicion as she comes from a part of Alabama that stayed loyal to the North during the Civil War – even though it was sixty years earlier!

SCOUT AND JEM'S RELATIONSHIP

Jem and Scout are obviously close, but their relationship is starting to change a little. Although Jem doesn't mind taking his little sister to school on her first day, he is quick to point out that Scout should 'leave him alone' (Chapter 2, p. 22) while there.

Scout is more impulsive and hot-headed than Jem, who is more responsible and mature. Jem's social manners are also more developed than Scout's.

However, they are fond of each other (at the end of Chapter 3, Scout sweetly brings supplies to Jem in the treehouse, for example), and they are affectionate even when teasing and criticising each other, such as when Scout mocks Jem's boasts of bravery.

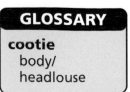

EXAMINER'S TIP: WRITING ABOUT EDUCATION

These chapters force us to think about education. We are invited to look at the different styles of teaching displayed by Scout's teachers – not only Miss Caroline but also Jem, Calpurnia and Atticus.

When Miss Caroline scolds a pupil for already knowing what she is expecting to teach, Harper Lee is poking fun at the state education system. Miss Caroline seems to have no understanding of the children as individuals, reading them stories they cannot relate to.

Scout learns a lesson from Calpurnia on social manners – that it is important to be tolerant of other people's ways and speech even though they may be different from one's own – and the moral is also passed on to the reader. This frequently used technique is employed when Atticus teaches Scout that you cannot fully understand someone until you look at things from his or her point of view – a key concept in the novel. Both Calpurnia and Atticus are trying to teach the children tolerance. They are very good at linking concrete events and examples to lessons they want them to learn.

? DID YOU KNOW

There are no black children at Scout's school.

CHECKPOINT 2

How are Miss Caroline's teaching methods different from Atticus's?

KEY QUOTE

Atticus: 'You never really understand a person ... until you climb into his skin and walk around in it' (Chapter 3, p. 35).

GLOSSARY

cootie body/headlouse

Chapters 4–6: The fascination continues

SUMMARY

❶ Scout and Jem discover gifts hidden in a tree knot-hole and wonder who has left them there.

❷ Scout rolls in a tyre, pushed by Jem, into the Radley Place steps.

❸ The children take on character roles – Dill's 'worst performance was Gothic' (Chapter 4, p. 45) – in a 'Boo Radley' play. They are caught by Atticus but deny the Radley connection.

❹ Scout spends time with Miss Maudie, who tells her more about the Radley family.

❺ Jem, Dill and Scout leave Boo a note. Atticus catches them and tells them off.

❻ The children try to see Boo Radley through the window. A shadow scares them and they run away to the sound of a shotgun. Jem loses his trousers on the fence, and later that night returns to retrieve them.

WHY ARE THESE CHAPTERS IMPORTANT?

A As Jem works out that Boo has left the gifts, we see the gap of understanding between Jem and Scout.

B Harper Lee uses the **narrator's** naivety to communicate information to the reader and also for the purpose of humour.

C We learn about Miss Maudie Atkinson and our understanding of the character of Atticus is deepened.

D The persona of Boo Radley is further expanded, and the Radley Place is vividly described. Miss Maudie gives an alternative perspective on Boo.

E The racial prejudice is alluded to further. The neighbours presume that the intruder in the Radleys' yard is black (Chapter 6, p. 60), showing how black people were often scapegoats, automatically linked with crimes.

THE NARRATOR'S NAIVETY AND ITS PURPOSE

Although Scout is the narrator, she does not always fully understand things. For example, she wrongly thinks Miss Maudie accuses Atticus of drinking whisky. She also misunderstands what Miss Maudie tells her about her conversation with Miss Stephanie.

As well as showing her innocence, Scout's naivety provides an opportunity for humour. The narrator's awareness is limited – she is not omniscient (all-knowing).

Harper Lee uses this narrative technique effectively: the voice of the mature narrator helps the reader bridge this gap of understanding, while allowing us still to enjoy Scout's refreshing childish perspective.

THE CHARACTERS OF ATTICUS AND MISS MAUDIE

We see what a fair person Atticus is. Even though he suspects that the children's game is connected with the Radleys, he lets it go because they deny it and he has no proof; perhaps his behaviour is more representative of a lawyer than of most parents? When Atticus finds the children trying to give Boo a note he tells them that it wasn't kind 'putting his life's history on display for the edification of the neighbourhood' (Chapter 5, p. 55), and again relates the scolding to the children's own situation, asking them how they would like it if he barged in on them without knocking.

How believable is Atticus's behaviour? Scout stands up for her father, when she wrongly assumes Miss Maudie is criticising him, and Miss Maudie clarifies by saying: 'Atticus Finch is the same in his house as he is on the public streets' (Chapter 5, p. 52). This implies to the reader that Atticus is very straightforward, with no hidden agenda.

Like Atticus, Miss Maudie is unusually open-minded and liberal compared to most of Maycomb's residents. Unlike Miss Stephanie and Mrs Dubose, she is friendly and tolerant. Miss Maudie is an important role model for Scout, who has no mother. She is described as a 'chameleon lady', who gardens in her coveralls, but who later appears dressed up as a lady in 'magisterial beauty' (Chapter 5, p. 48).

We wonder if Miss Maudie expresses Harper Lee's own opinions, when she indicates that the Bible can't be taken too literally and says that some people are 'so busy worrying about the next world they've never learned to live in this one' (Chapter 5, p. 51).

CHECKPOINT 3

Why are Atticus's words so effective? What earlier quotation does this remind you of?

EXAMINER'S TIP: WRITING ABOUT LANGUAGE – THE RADLEY PLACE

As well as remembering the plot, it is useful to make a note of how the writer uses language to create **atmosphere**. For instance, look at the description of the Radley Place in Chapter 6 and consider how the sinister mood is built up.

When the children try to look in the house, we see how Harper Lee establishes the tense atmosphere through language – Jem 'beckoning in the moonlight', the gate that 'squeaked', the 'ramshackle porch', the old stove and the mirror that 'caught the moon and shone eerily' (p. 58). The haunted house image is further developed through the hanging shutters, the lights peeping out from the curtains and the steps squeaking. We see the children's panic and rapid movement in words like 'leaped', 'galloped', 'flung', 'tripped' and 'dived' (p. 59).

The author shows her talent for creating atmosphere through her careful choice of language.

GLOSSARY

Gothic a nineteenth-century style that emphasised the horrific and paranormal
edification improvement

Chapters 7–8: Everyone to help

SUMMARY

❶ Jem and Scout find more things in the tree.

❷ The children try to leave a thank-you letter, and discover Mr Nathan Radley, Boo's keeper, filling up the hole.

❸ A cold winter brings heavy snow to Maycomb, as heavy as the 'Appomattox' (Mr Avery, Chapter 8, p. 71). Scout and Jem's snowman is 'an absolute morphodite' (Miss Maudie, Chapter 8, p. 74).

❹ Miss Maudie's house catches fire. Boo, unnoticed by the children, places a blanket around Scout's shoulders.

❺ Jem realises the blanket came from Boo and tells Atticus what's happened. Initially, Scout does not understand why.

WHY ARE THESE CHAPTERS IMPORTANT?

A   Jem's maturity and growing understanding are highlighted by his response to events.

B   The school system is ridiculed further when Scout tells us that her second year is even worse – 'they still flashed cards at you and wouldn't let you read or write' (Chapter 7, p. 64).

C   Attitutes towards black people in Maycomb are reiterated when Jem and Scout make a mudman covered with snow.

D   Miss Maudie's reaction to her house being destroyed tells us more about her character, not typically concerned by material goods.

E   The author continues the **theme** of doing the right thing.

F   We are reminded how small Maycomb is.

CHECKPOINT 4

Consider Mr Nathan Radley's action. This is the first time in the novel something innocent is punished unnecessarily. Why is he doing this?

❓ DID YOU KNOW

It is **ironic** that the snowman resembles Mr Avery, whose behaviour, unlike that of the black people in the story, is far from admirable.

KEY QUOTE

Miss Maudie shows courage (a recurring theme of the novel) and humour when she says, 'Always wanted a smaller house, Jem Finch. Gives me more yard' (Chapter 8, p. 79).

DOING THE RIGHT THING – AND BIRD IMAGERY

The title, bearing the mockingbird **motif**, threads through the novel, with bird imagery **symbolising** both sensing and doing the right thing.

The 'Finches', Jem and Scout, are taught by their father always to stand up for what is good and honest, and in these chapters Jem seems to be learning this lesson.

When the house fire starts, Scout says, 'Just as the birds know where to go when it rains, I knew when there was trouble in our street' (Chapter 8, pp. 74–5). We need to be aware of this continuing bird imagery as the novel progresses.

MAYCOMB'S SMALL COMMUNITY

The town seems very small and insular at times. When the telephone operator calls, for instance, we learn how many jobs she alone does.

Maycomb's infrastructure and services are quite fragile, as demonstrated the night of the fire when the Maycomb fire engine breaks down and the town has to get help from outside. Atticus says to the children, 'Looks like all of Maycomb was out tonight' (Chapter 8, p. 78).

The fire forces the community to wake from a deep sleep to tackle an alien situation, and can be seen as **symbolic** of the conflicts that the community will soon encounter (when Tom Robinson's case comes to trial). An event such as this also helps us, as modern readers with very different political attitudes and ideas, relate to the past.

EXAMINER'S TIP: WRITING ABOUT JEM'S CHARACTER

As Harper Lee's story unfolds, her characters become increasingly vivid enabling the reader to identify with them. Jem is obviously moved to discover that Boo has mended and folded his trousers and this challenges him to reassess his previous assumptions and prejudices – an indication of his growing up.

He realises that the dolls in the knot-hole have been carved by someone who knows well what the children look like. His decision to write a thank-you letter for the gifts shows his growing compassion for another human being. When Mr Radley tries to stop Boo's attempts to be friendly, this makes Jem sad. After the fire we see how Jem has shifted from being scared of Boo to being protective of him.

When Jem suddenly tells Atticus about Boo, Scout clearly does not understand the reason for his confessions and observations, saying he 'seemed to have lost his mind' (Chapter 8, p. 78).

? DID YOU KNOW

Over the years, bird **imagery** has been used by many writers including Shakespeare (Macbeth: 'the raven himself is hoarse').

★ GRADE BOOSTER

By discovering the appeal for today's readers, you may be awarded extra marks.

GLOSSARY

Appomattox the last battle of the Civil War; when the Southerners were finally defeated

absolute morphodite hermaphrodites have both male and female characteristics (the snowman resembles both Mr Avery and Miss Maudie)

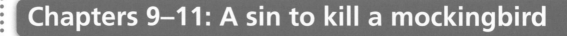

Chapters 9–11: A sin to kill a mockingbird

SUMMARY

❶ Atticus has taken on a court case in which he will defend a black man called Tom Robinson.

❷ Jem and Scout must learn self-control in the face of accusations against their father.

❸ The children are given air-rifles for Christmas.

❹ Atticus shoots a mad dog.

❺ Jem attacks Mrs Dubose's camellia bushes after her offensive remarks.

❻ Jem has to read to Mrs Dubose every night for a month, and before her death she leaves a single white camellia for him.

WHY ARE THESE CHAPTERS IMPORTANT?

A   Harper Lee introduces us to Tom Robinson and we learn more about the black community.

B   The message that it is important to hear two sides of an argument, not to make assumptions and to fight for one's beliefs, is reinforced.

C   We get to know Aunt Alexandra, and Scout is made to think about her femininity for the first time: 'I could not possibly hope to be a lady if I wore breeches' (Chapter 9, p. 87).

D   The mockingbird **motif** is referred to.

E   The children learn an important lesson about courage.

F   We learn more about Atticus and the stereotype of the 'Southern gentleman'.

G   The children discover that adults sometimes have to do things they do not want to do.

TOM ROBINSON AND THE BLACK COMMUNITY

Atticus tells Scout that he has taken on a 'peculiar case'. Calpurnia knows the family of the defendant well, and has said that 'they're clean-living folks' (Chapter 9, p. 81). Atticus respects Calpurnia and, as we have been encouraged to respect both **characters**, this directs positive feelings towards Tom Robinson, who, up to now, we have been told little about.

Atticus's comment, 'Why reasonable people go stark raving mad when anything involving a [black person] comes up, is something I don't pretend to understand' (Chapter 9, pp. 94–5), tells us first-hand how he feels about the trial.

In Chapter 10, Zeebo, the local rubbish collector, comes to collect the mad dog. We will learn in Chapter 12 that he is one of the few black people there who can read. This tells us a lot about the position of black people in this society and their job opportunities, or lack of them.

Mrs Dubose's racism is particularly **ironic**, as she was very dependent on her black servant Jessie. In 1930s America it was common for white people to have black servants.

CHECKPOINT 5

What could the flower-gift symbolise?

KEY QUOTE

Atticus: 'Shoot all the bluejays you want, if you can hit 'em, but remember it's a sin to kill a mockingbird' (Chapter 10, p. 96).

ATTICUS AND THE 'SOUTHERN GENTLEMAN' STEREOTYPE

Initially, Jem and Scout believe their father is not 'macho' enough. They describe him as 'feeble', saying 'he never went hunting, he did not play poker or fish or drink or smoke. He sat in the living-room and read'. To them, his work in an office meant he 'didn't do anything' (Chapter 10, p. 95).

Harper Lee is breaking down the stereotype of the Southern gentleman (see **Key theme: Prejudice**). When Atticus shoots the mad dog in Chapter 10, his children's appreciation of him increases. It is a crucial time to have gained the children's respect – just before the trial.

We need to consider the **symbolism** and irony of the mad dog incident. Atticus is protecting the community from something dangerous. Is he later able to protect something innocent from the madness of the community? With the dog called 'Tim Johnson', a name not dissimilar to 'Tom Robinson', we realise that Harper Lee wants us to draw some parallels between this incident and the trial.

Also in Chapter 10 we learn that Atticus has a problem with his left eye. This links him to Tom, who has a weakened left arm, and is perhaps one of the reasons Atticus is able to work out later that Tom was unlikely to have been the man who hurt Mayella Ewell.

EXAMINER'S TIP: WRITING ABOUT FIGHTING FOR YOUR BELIEFS

Structurally, through these last chapters of Part One the author gives us important background details for Part Two, with several incidents preparing the reader for the trial scenes to come.

Scout becomes angry with Uncle Jack for punishing her before hearing her side of the story. Later on we will feel a similar sympathy for Tom Robinson when his side of the story is not believed.

Atticus knows he has little chance of winning the case as African-Americans do not have the same rights or position in this society as whites; it is just a 'black man's word against the Ewells' '. But he explains that he has to do what is right: 'do you think I could face my children otherwise?' (Chapter 9, p. 94).

The **theme** of courage is explored widely in these chapters. In Chapter 11 Atticus speaks of 'real courage' as 'when you know you're licked before you begin but you begin anyway and you see it through no matter what' (p. 118). His comments relate to both Mrs Dubose and himself at the forthcoming trial.

GRADE BOOSTER

Scout is eavesdropping when she overhears talk about the trial. The author uses such techniques to allow us to hear adult conversations first-hand. However, you could argue that if Scout were present too often, we would become too aware of authorial purpose and the story might seem contrived.

DID YOU KNOW

The author is using the technique of **foreshadowing** in these scenes.

EXAMINER'S TIP

The theme of courage is a strong one in the novel. Build up quotes under main theme headings. This can make life easier for you when you revise and write essays.

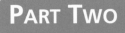

PART TWO

Chapters 12–14: 'Fine folks'

SUMMARY

❶ Jem is twelve years old and is growing up.

❷ Calpurnia takes Jem and Scout to the black people's church.

❸ We learn about Tom Robinson's family and that he is accused of rape.

❹ Aunt Alexandra comes to stay and persuades Atticus to try to make his children appreciate that they 'are not from run-of-the-mill people' (Chapter 13, p. 139).

❺ Aunt Alexandra and Atticus quarrel about Calpurnia's position in the household.

❻ Dill turns up, having run away from his home in Mississippi.

GRADE BOOSTER

You could argue that the naive position of the **narrator** is a useful way for Harper Lee to provide the reader with explanations and definitions, such as when Scout asks Atticus what rape is.

WHY ARE THESE CHAPTERS IMPORTANT?

A We learn more about the black community, the Robinson family and other key figures.

B The reader views a boy's rite of passage – given as Jem moves from childhood towards adulthood.

C The author provides further information about the forthcoming trial.

D Traditional family views of some Southern people are explored and we see how it may be difficult to bring about change in such an 'inward' community (Chapter 13, p. 137).

E We see how Dill's unhappy experiences contrast with the unquestioning love felt by the Finch children.

DID YOU KNOW

The discussion at the end of Chapter 14 emphasises an important message from the author – that making a child feel secure and wanted is more important than material possessions.

THE BLACK COMMUNITY

It is appropriate that one episode should take place in a church as we have previously learnt that all the main events of Maycomb are centred around church activities. In Chapter 12 we find out much more about the black community, its community care, dignity and also about Tom Robinson's family. The children learn, for instance, that only four people in Calpurnia's church can read. Scout and Jem are clearly unaware that the black population is denied an education.

Lula May is the only black character with any 'negative' characteristics. Critics have said the lack of such characters makes the novel unrealistic. However, at the time black people could not outwardly show their disapproval of white people's ways, for fear of prejudice and losing their jobs. Therefore, perhaps it is **realistic** that discontent is shown when a white child breaks the very rules of segregation that white people had imposed.

Atticus shows Calpurnia the highest respect, while Aunt Alexandra treats her very differently – reminding us of how black people were typically treated at this time before we enter the trial period.

TRADITIONAL FAMILY BACKGROUND

The children's discussion with Aunt Alexandra about the definition of 'fine folks' (Chapter 13, p. 135) is an interesting and amusing one, and they obviously do not understand her concern with family and heritage.

It is **ironic** that Aunt Alexandra wants the children to appreciate their family background, characterised as it was by slavery, when it is the freedom of a black man that Atticus is fighting for. The children know little about the Finch family history and we get the impression that Atticus would prefer them to form their own views about the world and not take on family airs and graces.

EXAMINER'S TIP: WRITING ABOUT JEM GROWING UP

Part One ends with the writer showing Jem's hot-headed actions and with him having to learn some important lessons. Part Two begins with Jem entering adolescence, with mood swings, an 'appalling' appetite and 'an alien set of values' (Chapter 12, p. 121). Scout finds it hard to relate to her brother, who now tells her 'It's time you started bein' a girl and acting right!' (Chapter 12, p. 121). These changes are also marked by Atticus telling Scout to give Jem space and by Calpurnia now calling him 'Mister Jem' (Chapter 12, p. 121).

In Chapter 14 Jem gets into a fight with Scout and Atticus has to intervene. Jem later tells Atticus about Dill's arrival. This shows his fluctuating adult and childlike behaviour (see **Key theme: Growing up**).

Both Jem and Scout are learning from Atticus that moral issues can be complicated. This makes growing up more of a challenge for Jem, but ultimately will make him more sensitive and thoughtful.

EXAMINER'S TIP

Think about how and when the author presents information to the reader. For instance, we have heard only positive things about Tom Robinson and negative things about the Ewells, so we are therefore naturally more inclined to sympathise with Tom before the trial even begins.

KEY QUOTE

Scout (narrator): 'Jem ... broke the remaining code of our childhood' (Chapter 14, p. 146).

GRADE BOOSTER

Although you are discussing Jem here, referring to Scout in passing shows you are appreciating a wider perspective.

Chapters 15–17: Calming the mob & The trial begins

SUMMARY

CHECKPOINT 6

How does Scout learn the information Heck Tate tells Atticus?

❶ The sheriff informs Atticus that they are moving Tom Robinson to the Maycomb jail and that there may be problems.

❷ Jem, Scout and Dill find Atticus outside the jail and the lynch mob forms around him.

❸ Scout spots Mr Cunningham and talks to him, which results in the crowd dispersing.

❹ Atticus explains to Scout that people's behaviour changes when they are part of a mob.

❺ People from all around Maycomb arrive for the trial and Dill is told about the various characters. Miss Maudie says she will not attend this 'carnival' (Chapter 16, p. 165).

❻ In the courthouse the children cannot find anywhere to sit until Reverend Sykes offers them seats in the black people's balcony.

❼ The trial begins with Heck Tate's testimony. He states that Mayella's right eye was badly bruised. Robert Ewell is then questioned.

WHY ARE THESE CHAPTERS IMPORTANT?

CHECKPOINT 7

Note the reference again to standing in another's shoes. Who stood? In whose shoes?

A When Scout speaks to Mr Cunningham, she unknowingly appeals to his humanity and prevents an unpleasant situation occurring. Scout is unconsciously pointing out a moral to the men – that it is a sin to kill a mockingbird (Atticus/Tom Robinson).

B Symbolism is used in descriptions, the view of the clock tower 'indicating a people determined to preserve every physical scrap of the past' (Chapter 16, p. 168).

C The description of characters provides a backdrop to the trial.

D The author re-emphasises the segregation between black and white people.

E The tone of the first part of the trial is set with the questioning of Mayella's father.

EXAMINER'S TIP

If you mention, in relation to the many people arriving, that town trials were big social events in America in the 1930s, it can reveal your knowledge of the historical background and different culture.

DILL AND THE CHARACTERS OF MAYCOMB

It was important that Dill returned in Chapter 14. This allows the writer to use the narrative device of Jem describing to him (and thus the reader) the various well-known characters coming to the trial, as was the case previously when Dill was told about the Radleys and Maycomb. Dill hears about Mr Dolphus Raymond, for instance, who is shunned by the white community for living with and having children by a black woman – Jem describes the children as 'in-betweens' who 'don't belong anywhere' (Chapter 16, p. 167).

Look at Scout's remark 'Well if we came out durin' the Old Testament it's too long ago to matter' (Chapter 16, p. 168) in the context of the conversation about whether they could have black ancestors. Although the children are not racially prejudiced in a conventional way, they have still picked up some of the beliefs and stereotypes from their community. This includes their initial view of Dolphus Raymond.

RACIAL SEGREGATION

The segregation of the black and white population in Maycomb is highlighted by the way the black people file into court last and are seated in the balcony. Their politeness towards Jem, Scout and Dill is again shown when people give up their front seats for them. This also implies that in this society white children have priority over black adults. It is **ironic** that the children will have the same viewpoint as the black people during the trial – both in population terms of what they see and where they see it from.

If we compare the description of where the Ewells live with the description of the black settlement (Chapter 17, pp. 176–7), we can see that Harper Lee is subtly giving us impressions about these characters through an examination of their home environment.

DID YOU KNOW

In 1930s America, where a key ideal was working hard to earn your living and to attain your status without depending too much on any government body for support, characters like the Ewells would have been strongly criticised.

EXAMINER'S TIP: WRITING ABOUT QUESTIONING ROBERT EWELL 🔓

Having been given useful information about the Ewell family in previous chapters, we are not surprised by the rather unattractive description of Robert Ewell and his family. We are told that 'No economic fluctuations changed their status – people like the Ewells lived as guests of the county in prosperity as well as in the depths of a depression' (Chapter 17, p. 176).

When questioned by Mr Gilmer (who is representing Mayella Ewell), Robert Ewell is provoked into using such bad language that court proceedings are interrupted. Later, his left-handedness is revealed to the court by Atticus. Ewell does not understand language such as 'ambidextrous' (Chapter 17, p. 184), nor does he understand the significance of Atticus's questions. In contrast, Scout, an articulate child with an understanding of legal language, uses terms such as 'circuit solicitor' (Chapter 17, p. 172) in her narration.

Ewell does not see that his failure to get a doctor indicates his lack of care for his family and possible guilt, and that his left-handedness suggests he could have been responsible for causing the injuries on the right side of Mayella's face. Yet, even though he offends the African-American audience by his language, the white crowd is somewhat entertained by his attitude.

Had we not been given the background on the Maycomb characters and the racial discrimination previously, we, like Jem, would presume at this first stage of the trial that Atticus was winning the case.

DID YOU KNOW

It is perhaps ironic that Robert Ewell – a white man – is asked to prove his literacy, and that the act of writing with his left hand hints at his guilt. In the time of slavery, if it was discovered that a black man could write he was punished and sometimes his right hand was cut off.

GLOSSARY

ambidextrous the ability to use both hands equally well

circuit solicitor a lawyer who works within a defined regional area

Chapters 18–19: Mayella versus Tom

SUMMARY

❶ Mayella Ewell is questioned by Mr Gilmer and Atticus and has difficulties answering and giving evidence.

❷ Atticus asks Mayella to be sure she has got the right man and she gets confused, eventually bursting into tears for the second time and refusing to say more.

❸ Jem notices that Tom has a weakened left arm and hand.

❹ Tom Robinson takes the stand and Atticus questions him on his version of events, after which Mr Gilmer questions him.

❺ Mr Link Deas, who used to employ Tom, speaks for his defence out of turn and is sent out the room, adding to the courtroom drama.

GRADE BOOSTER

Although Mayella's mistake can later be seen as unforgivable, you could argue that a painting such a picture of her sad background means that we feel sympathy and can therefore also relate to the sympathy that Tom felt for Mayella.

WHY ARE THESE CHAPTERS IMPORTANT?

A Atticus's questions to Mayella build up a picture of her poor and deprived life. There are indications that she has tried to rise above her squalid living conditions, and therefore her mistake hurts her personal pride.

B Tom's answers reveal his honesty, good nature, kindness and sensitivity and we learn that it is impossible for him to have committed the crime in the way it was described.

C We see the discrepancies between Mayella's and Tom's stories.

D The use of language by the main **characters** is revealing.

E We see that the accepted traits for a Southern gentleman are not regarded by most people in the community as appropriate traits for a black man to display.

TOM'S VERSION OF EVENTS AGAINST MAYELLA'S

The fact that one version of events follows the other in these chapters helps the reader to identify discrepancies more easily.

Notice where the 'chiffarobe' (Chapter 18, p. 186; Chapter 19, p. 197) appears in the two versions. It is clear that Tom would not say that he had helped Mayella previously if he had not, as it would do nothing to help his case – Mayella had stated that this was the first time she had called for his help.

It seems that the position of black people in the American South in the 1930s spells doom for Tom Robinson. Whichever way he had acted in response to the advances of a white woman – defending himself or running away – would have been perceived as guilt. He is caught.

'YOU FELT SORRY FOR HER'

When asked why he did odd jobs for Mayella for no money, Tom states that he saw that she was struggling. He is very careful not to say that Mayella was lying. However, when he says he felt sorry for her, Mr Gilmer picks up on this, stating, 'You felt sorry for *her*, you felt *sorry* for her?' (Chapter 19, p. 203).

Tom has overstepped some societal boundaries and his admission of sympathy for Mayella – a white woman – is considered impertinent due to the lower status of black people at that time.

Tom has embarrassed the Ewells, as well as revealing in his testimony that Bob Ewell sexually abuses his daughter.

EXAMINER'S TIP: WRITING ABOUT CHARACTERS' LANGUAGE

Harper Lee comments on the different characters, both as the adult narrator and through the child Scout's observations, but she uses a clever technique to do so, which allows the reader to judge for themselves. We witness direct speech and hear the speakers' own use of language, and thereby 'meet' the characters and form our own opinions of them.

Tom uses very polite language, not wishing to repeat in court Robert Ewell's bad language or to say that Mayella is lying but instead repeating 'she's mistaken in her mind' (Chapter 19, p. 204).

Mayella, in contrast, does not understand Atticus's polite language and when he calls her 'Ma'am' says to Judge Taylor, 'I don't hafta take his sass' (Chapter 18, p. 188). She is evidently not used to a man treating her with courtesy and presumes that Atticus is mocking her.

Mr Gilmer doesn't give Tom the same respect, addressing him patronisingly as 'boy' (Chapter 19, p. 203).

EXAMINER'S TIP

By discussing the author's positioning of events, you can display knowledge of the role of structure in the novel.

KEY QUOTE

The sexual abuse is alluded to when Tom quotes Mayella as saying that 'what her papa do to her don't count' (Chapter 19, p. 200).

GLOSSARY

chiffarobe wardrobe
take his sass accept his insult

Chapters 20–1: The verdict

SUMMARY

❶ Scout has left the courthouse with Dill, as he is feeling unwell. They talk to Dolphus Raymond.

❷ Dill and Scout return to the courtroom to hear Atticus conclude his defence of Tom Robinson.

❸ Several hours later, the jury presents its verdict: Tom Robinson is guilty.

❹ The black people stand as Atticus leaves the courtroom.

WHY ARE THESE CHAPTERS IMPORTANT?

A Atticus states clearly that all the trial comes down to is a question of race.

B Dill's character becomes more rounded, as he shows his innocence and his sensitivity to the trial's events.

C Dolphus Raymond's conversation with Dill and Scout forms an important interlude, and gives us the opportunity to consider further issues about race.

D The long-awaited trial is at last finished and we hear the concluding arguments and then the verdict – arguably the heart of *To Kill a Mockingbird*.

THE INNOCENCE OF CHILDREN

Dill shows his innocence when he and Scout talk to Dolphus Raymond and when he drinks from Dolphus's paper sack. We appreciate that it is a shame adults lose this innocence as by innocently entering into such an encounter children's prejudices can be broken down. Jem and Scout's optimism about Atticus winning shows how all the evidence points to Tom's innocence and how they don't have the rigid, adult prejudices that prevent the jury from honouring the truth.

Children judge things by 'natural' justice. The theme of the innocence of children is referred to by Atticus after the lynch mob scene and again later as they discuss the trial (Chapter 16, p. 163; Chapter 22, p. 219). It is also echoed by Dolphus Raymond, who says he tells them about his 'perpetrated fraud' (Chapter 20, p. 207) because they are children and can understand it.

We see from such comments, as well as from Harper Lee's **epigraph** – 'Lawyers, I suppose, were children once' (Charles Lamb) – how important this idea was to the author. Perhaps this is one of the many reasons Harper Lee's novel has been such a success – because she captures that childhood innocence we can all personally recognise and appreciate. She is perhaps implying that however important the role or job is that we take on in later life, we should try to remember the world we viewed as a child, free from prejudice.

THE OUTCOME OF THE TRIAL

As Atticus brings his arguments to the jury to a close, he emphasises again that no evidence has been produced to convict Tom Robinson, and in fact much to the contrary. Mayella, he says, felt guilt as she broke a 'code' and 'did something that in our society is unspeakable: she kissed a black man' (Chapter 20, pp. 209–10).

Although Atticus has pity for Mayella, he says this is not enough to justify her 'putting a man's life at stake' (Chapter 20, p. 209). He reminds the jury of the statement by 'Thomas Jefferson' (Chapter 20, p. 211) that all men are created equal and pleads with them to do their duty. He is inviting the jury to have the courage to question their preconceived attitudes and beliefs.

When the jury returns to give its verdict, Scout **narrates** that she saw something that 'only a lawyer's child could be expected to see ... A jury never looks at a defendant it has convicted, and when this jury came in, not one of them looked at Tom Robinson' (Chapter 21, p. 217).

Despite strong and persuasive arguments, Tom Robinson is declared guilty. Racial prejudice is still too strong, and this society is not yet able to deal with such a case appropriately. As readers we can feel sad, but Harper Lee prepares us for this by all the previous descriptions of Maycomb's history and inhabitants.

GRADE BOOSTER

In your arguments, referring to any **symbolism** used by the author can be effective – for instance, the quiet, ominous feeling in the courtroom when the jury returns is like 'a cold February morning, when the mockingbirds were still' (Chapter 21, p. 216).

EXAMINER'S TIP: WRITING ABOUT MEETING DOLPHUS RAYMOND

The interlude with Dolphus Raymond at the beginning of Chapter 20 gives the reader a breathing space from the intensity of the trial and **foreshadows** Atticus's views, expressed later, that black people are people like everyone else.

Through meeting Dolphus and discovering that it is Coca-Cola rather than whisky that he drinks, we learn that we shouldn't judge by appearances. Although Scout judges Dolphus initially by his reputation, her opinion changes after she has met him – something that sadly the white jury of the trial is not able to do regarding Tom Robinson.

This scene underlines the prejudices of the white community, with hints that if a white person loves a black person they have to have an excuse for it and with Scout learning more about the 'simple hell people give other people' (Chapter 20, p. 207).

Dolphus Raymond's 'fraud' is one way in which society copes with threats to its established norms. Mayella's guilty denial could be seen as another.

GLOSSARY

Thomas Jefferson the man who wrote the Declaration of Independence after the United States of America was formed, on which the government is based

Chapters 22–3: Following the trial

SUMMARY

❶ Jem is very upset by the trial result.

❷ Atticus is moved to discover that many black people have left him gifts of food.

❸ Miss Maudie offers support and acknowledges that Jem is growing up.

❹ Bob Ewell spits at Atticus and threatens to kill him.

❺ Jem says he thinks there are four types of people in the world, while Scout suggests there is only one.

WHY ARE THESE CHAPTERS IMPORTANT?

A We see that the black community is grateful for Atticus's tough defence of Tom Robinson.

B The incident with Bob Ewell maintains some tension in the story, keeping the reader's interest.

C The children's education continues, and Jem's growing-up is highlighted.

D We learn some of Atticus's personal views regarding the trial.

E Harper Lee again emphasises the innocence of children compared to adults when Atticus responds to Jem's complaint about Tom's conviction: 'You couldn't, but they could and did' (Chapter 23, p. 227).

GRADE BOOSTER

By referring back to the trial, you can display your in-depth knowledge of the novel.

CHECKPOINT 8

Look at Scout and Jem's different views. What are the 'four types' of people and what is the 'one type'? Which view do you agree with most?

CHECKPOINT 9

What does Atticus's language remind you of?

THE REACTION TO THE VERDICT

The children have been closely involved with the trial and it has had a big impact on them. Jem is clearly very angry and upset, and needs to try to work things out rationally. Dill responds by saying he will one day become a clown – a new kind of clown who laughs at people – thus separating himself from other people of Maycomb, in particular his Aunt Rachel for whom he has lost all respect towards.

Atticus makes Jem realise that juries are not always guided by reason. However, he also points out that he should not be disheartened as they intend to appeal. After Robert Ewell's attack Atticus maintains that the children should try to see things from Ewell's point of view.

GROWING UP

Miss Maudie provides a motherly perspective, and offers Jem a slice of the adult cake in recognition of his age. This is **symbolic** of a kind of rite of passage.

Jem is becoming more aware of life's harsh realities. He suddenly understands how things may seem from Boo's point of view. We get the impression that Harper Lee is putting forward a moral argument that children should not be shielded from society's realities but must be given the tools to deal with the environment in which they live.

As we observe the children's growth, we wonder whether other characters have had to grow through these times. For instance, Scout notices Aunt Alexandra calling Atticus 'brother', showing an empathy that was not apparent earlier. As Miss Maudie says to Jem at the end of Chapter 22, the trial has had an impact on everyone: 'it's just a baby-step, but it's a step' (p. 222).

EXAMINER'S TIP: WRITING ABOUT ATTICUS'S VIEWS ON THE TRIAL

Atticus's words to Jem about the trial reveal his outrage (see Chapter 23, p. 227). Although the effect on the reader is powerful, when looking closely at Atticus's words we see how even a very unusually enlightened man is affected by the standard 'white' perception of black people's 'ignorance'. Although he is sympathetic and tolerant, Atticus could not completely step into a black man's skin (see **Key theme: Prejudice**).

It is important to consider the views commonly held at the time from a modern perspective. Atticus is a man of his time. His view is slightly restricted – that the race issue will only be solved by white people changing their attitudes rather than taking into consideration the actions that black people themselves will take.

Atticus finds it difficult to explain society's prejudice to the children. He uses legal language such as 'commutes his sentence', 'straight acquittal' and 'hung jury' (Chapter 23, pp. 225, 229) to talk about the inadequacies of the legal system and about prejudice against black people. He points out that a Cunningham on the jury had been convinced of Tom Robinson's innocence. Atticus's comments on this member of the jury – along with the jury's long deliberations and Mr Underwood's newspaper article – could be considered one of the most optimistic notes of the novel: Atticus had managed to make a man from a prejudiced family stop and think for a moment and this was 'the shadow of a beginning' (Chapter 23, p. 228).

CHECKPOINT 10

What is Atticus trying to get the children to do again? Look at your previous answers about standing in other people's shoes.

GLOSSARY

commutes his sentence reduces the severity of his sentence

straight acquittal immediate release

hung jury where the jury cannot reach a clear decision acceptable for sentencing, i.e. two dissenters out of twelve

Chapters 24–6: Tom's death

SUMMARY

❶ Aunt Alexandra is entertaining the Maycomb Missionary Society. They have a discussion about race, which Miss Maudie angrily brings to an end.

❷ Atticus learns that Tom Robinson has been shot dead while trying to escape. He asks Calpurnia to accompany him to tell Helen, Tom's wife.

❸ Jem emphasises that it is wrong to kill creatures that do no harm.

❹ Mr Underwood reports Tom's death in *The Maycomb Tribune*, likening it to 'the senseless slaughter of songbirds' (Chapter 25, p. 247).

❺ A new school year begins. Scout is surprised when her teacher Miss Gates talks about Hitler's persecution of the Jews and contrasts it with the 'non-prejudiced' United States.

❻ Scout cannot understand Miss Gates as she had heard her speaking badly of black people to Miss Stephanie on her way out of the courthouse.

❼ Jem tells Scout not to talk of the courthouse again. Atticus later explains to the puzzled Scout that Jem needs to forget about the trial for a while.

WHY ARE THESE CHAPTERS IMPORTANT?

A The position of women is examined through the Missionary Society meeting.

B Tom's death finalises a period that has not really been closed. The **symbolism** of the mockingbird and the harming of innocent creatures reiterates how senseless Tom's death is.

C A different style of storytelling is used, rather than the **first-person narrative** that runs through the novel.

D We see that the children are no longer frightened of the Radley Place, and that Jem is still angry about the trial verdict.

E Harper Lee explores the **theme** of hypocrisy.

CHECKPOINT 11

Why do you think the songbird **theme** occurs again here?

KEY QUOTE

Scout quotes Miss Gates's words immediately after the trial: 'I heard her say it's time somebody taught 'em a lesson, they were gettin' way above them-selves, an' the next thing they think they can do is marry us' (Chapter 26, p. 253).

KEY CONNECTIONS

The final chapter of *Black Like Me* (1960) by John Howard Griffin documents race relations in the Civil Rights Movement. For historical documents of the Scottsboro trials and the Civil Rights Movement, check out *Understanding To Kill a Mockingbird* by Claudia Durst Johnson (1994).

MAYCOMB WOMEN

Scout attends a Missionary Society tea, and through her descriptions and observations we learn much about Southern womanhood at this time. The women are all uniformly dressed in their 'pastel prints' and 'smelled heavenly' (Chapter 24, p. 235). Scout appears to take interest in them when she states 'I must soon enter this world' (Chapter 24, p. 240).

Although Calpurnia and Miss Maudie have up until now been Scout's main female role models, we see that Aunt Alexandra's courteous behaviour after the news of Tom Robinson's death has an impact on Scout, as she says, 'if Aunty could be a lady at a time like this, so could I' (Chapter 24, p. 244).

We get the impression that Scout will never be quite like Aunt Alexandra, but she obviously wants her aunt to be pleased with her behaviour, and shows a new maturity.

MESSENGERS OF BAD NEWS

Dill tells Scout about the trip to see Helen Robinson. This is one of the few scenes where Scout is not present. The incident at the Robinsons' home is instead recounted as Scout remembers what Dill had told her.

Dill explains that Helen fell down when she learnt of her husband's death, 'like a giant with a big foot just came along and stepped on her' (Chapter 25, p. 246). This is a very effective **simile** as it highlights the way grief suddenly hits with full force.

Although this episode forms a refreshing contrast to Scout's first-hand accounts, it loses some immediacy in the retelling. We can therefore appreciate how the style of the first-person narrative gives a more vivid picture in the rest of the novel.

KEY QUOTE

Scout (narrator): 'I was more at home in my father's world' (Chapter 24, p. 240).

? DID YOU KNOW

Harper Lee uses Scout to make a statement about Southern womanhood and the status of women at the time. Using a child for this purpose is a subtle and unthreatening way of making a social comment.

EXAMINER'S TIP: WRITING ABOUT THE THEME OF HYPOCRISY

The theme of hypocrisy runs through the novel, but is very prominent in these chapters. The Missionary Society women's conversation is **ironic** and hypocritical: the subject of their talk is the plight of an African tribe, but these women have no concern for the African-Americans living in their own neighbourhood. Their attitudes are **satirised** when they talk about the tribe being 'one big family', mocking the Maycomb people's obsession with family names and the varying amount of status given to different families.

The news of Tom's death highlights how trivial the women's talk is (although it brings out an admirable and softer side to Aunt Alexandra's personality). We see how Harper Lee has purposefully juxtaposed (placed together) events for dramatic effect.

Scout is becoming increasingly able to juxtapose separate events herself. She later recognises the hypocrisy of her teacher speaking passionately against Hitler's cruelty towards the Jews when African-Americans in their own society are wrongly treated.

★ GRADE BOOSTER

If you use in your essays, where appropriate, the technique of juxtaposing two events to make an argument, adding quotes to back up your points, you may be awarded extra marks.

Atticus explains that Robert Ewell tried to burgle the judge's house because the judge had made him 'look like a fool', staring at him as if he were a 'three-legged chicken or a square egg' (Chapter 27, p. 256).

DID YOU KNOW

The fact that an outsider is initially blamed shows the paranoia local people now feel after their stability and safety have been shaken.

CHECKPOINT 12

What is the 'crunching'?

Chapters 27–9: Acts of revenge

SUMMARY

❶ Robert Ewell has a score to settle with Atticus, blaming him when he loses a new job.

❷ Judge Taylor's house is broken into, probably by Robert Ewell. Helen Robinson is also followed and threatened by Ewell. Mr Link Deas, who has given Helen work, has to warn Ewell to leave her alone.

❸ Misses Tutti and Frutti have their furniture moved to their cellar by some children, but initially blame an outsider.

❹ A Halloween pageant is organised and Scout is given the part of a ham.

❺ Cecil Jacobs jumps out on Jem and Scout, who are walking to the pageant. On the way home, they hear noises behind them and realise it is not a joke.

❻ Somebody attacks Scout. There is a big scuffle and she hears strange noises and a 'crunching sound' (Chapter 28, p. 268). Jem screams.

❼ A man staggers away, groaning. Scout finds a man on the ground who smells of whisky and someone carries Jem home.

❽ Heck Tate arrives, explaining that he has found Bob Ewell dead under the Radleys' tree. Mr Tate asks Scout what happened.

❾ At the end of her story, Scout points to the man in the corner who came to their rescue and realises this man is Boo.

WHY ARE THESE CHAPTERS IMPORTANT?

A The author uses these chapters to re-establish some normality in everyday life.

B The incident with Misses Tutti and Frutti allows for humour after the heavier tones of the trial scenes.

C We experience a certain sympathy with Aunt Alexandra's character that we did not imagine possible at the beginning.

D The Halloween event and pageant indicate the Maycomb inhabitants' need to bond and to honour their town's heritage, as well as the country's history, to heal any wounded pride. Notably, Atticus chooses not to attend.

E Dramatic tension and suspense lead up to Bob Ewell's attack on the children.

MAYCOMB RETURNS TO NORMALITY

After the events of the trial, Maycomb returns to normality. Scout reports everyday incidents such as the prank involving Misses Tutti and Frutti Barber's house, and these seem trivial following the drama of the trial.

Structurally, such 'normal' events are important in a novel with a documentary as well as a dramatic purpose (see **realism**), and a time of calm is necessary after the pace and tension of the trial chapters.

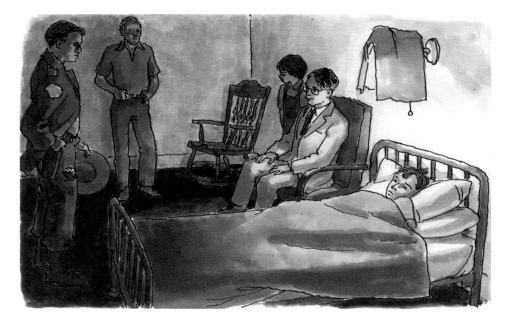

As we have seen, there are also personal reasons why **characters** may need to focus on everyday events.

THE DEVELOPMENT OF AUNT ALEXANDRA'S CHARACTER

Aunt Alexandra's humanity has been emerging since the trial scenes, with her concern for Atticus, her worthy demeanour at the news of Tom's death, and the great care she displays when the children are hurt – putting Scout's comfort before her own desire to turn her into a 'lady'.

Although Aunt Alexandra is arguably a prejudiced and difficult **character**, coming to live with the family when Atticus is involved in such a controversial trial could be seen as a very brave act.

It is a sign of Harper Lee's skill as a novelist that she doesn't make such characters two-dimensional, but can draw out many facets to their personality. She shows that even the most conservative characters may be capable of some development.

EXAMINER'S TIP: WRITING ABOUT DRAMATIC TENSION AND SUSPENSE

Harper Lee cleverly builds up suspense and tension – partly by comments and events and also by her use of language. The mention of Aunt Alexandra having a premonition before the pageant (Chapter 27, p. 260), as Jem did before the mob scene in Chapter 15 (p. 153), is an example of a small aside with later significance.

A feeling of suspense is created through the use of language in Chapter 28. The reference to the 'solitary mocker' (p. 261) at the beginning of the chapter foreshadows the mockingbird (Boo) appearing later.

The incident with Cecil is timely, as the reader expects danger but it turns out to be a prank. The author is cleverly building up the parallels. For instance, in one of the attractions at the pageant the children are made to touch objects that supposedly come from a human being. Thus when the Robert Ewell episode occurs later, and Scout unwittingly touches his dead body it is even more dramatic and sinister in contrast (see **Structure**).

Chapters 30–1: A private trial

SUMMARY

❶ Doctor Reynolds arrives at the Finches' house and examines Jem.

❷ Atticus, Heck Tate, Arthur (Boo) Radley and Scout go out onto the porch.

❸ Atticus does not understand why Heck is insisting that Bob Ewell fell on his knife and believes that the incident must go to court.

❹ He eventually understands that Heck is trying to protect Boo Radley's privacy.

❺ Scout takes Boo Radley in to see Jem. At Boo's request, Scout walks him home – the last she will see of him.

❻ Scout looks back at past incidents from Boo's point of view and contemplates Atticus's message: to understand someone you need to stand in their shoes.

❼ Scout joins Atticus beside the sleeping Jem and Atticus begins to read her *'The Grey Ghost'* (Chapter 31, p. 286). She soon falls asleep.

CHECKPOINT 14

Note the recurring mockingbird **motif**. Why could Jem also be linked to the mockingbird **theme** here?

EXAMINER'S TIP

By referring to how loose ends are tied up at the end of the novel, you can indicate your awareness of authorial purpose.

WHY ARE THESE CHAPTERS IMPORTANT?

A Bob Ewell is finally out of the picture, so no longer poses a threat. Now that Scout has finally seen Boo, all loose ends are tied up.

B Harper Lee makes the point again that the court system has its limitations.

C The novel's main themes – growing up, courage, prejudice – are emphasised and key **symbolism** is highlighted.

D Boo becomes known as a person, but is also given spiritual status.

E Although Scout has reached a new level of maturity, we are reminded when she falls asleep that she is after all still a little girl.

THE CHARACTER OF BOO

When Scout really sees Boo for the first time we are finally given a full physical description of him. This contrasts greatly with the children's idea of him in early chapters, and contains hints of the mockingbird: wide mouth, grey eyes, 'feathery' hair (Chapter 30, p. 279).

The fact that Scout treats Boo/Arthur Radley with some familiarity makes him seem normal. This is emphasised when she realises that Dr Reynolds has seen Boo before: 'Of course ... even Boo Radley got sick sometimes' (Chapter 30, p. 277). However, she does feel that having Boo there is slightly unreal.

Boo says nothing about the earlier incident, thus neither implicating nor absolving himself. This maintains his mysterious status persona. Heck Tate loses his temper with Atticus when he cannot see that the reason he wants to keep the incident quiet is not for Jem's sake but Boo's.

When Atticus says to Boo, as if in prayer, 'Thank you for my children, Arthur' (Chapter 30, p. 283), we note the religious overtones. This is echoed by Scout, as she looks back on events and summarises the story in a dream-like fashion, referring to herself and Jem as God's children. It seems that Boo has been watching over Scout and Jem throughout.

PRIVATE JUSTICE

We are never completely certain whether it was Jem or Boo who stabbed Bob Ewell. Harper Lee implies that the real issue here is the need to protect an innocent creature (Boo).

Heck Tate uses Bob Ewell's left-handedness (Chapter 30, p. 280) as evidence, in the same way that Atticus did in Tom's trial (see **Structure**).

Atticus is eventually persuaded that the public legal system is not suitable here, and that they must use their own rules and sense of justice. The legal system was not sufficient to save the other mockingbird of the story (Tom Robinson).

We do not know whether Scout has completely understood the adults' conversation or whether she has responded to repetition of the word 'sin' and linked it with Atticus's lesson in Chapter 10 – when the mockingbird is first introduced.

EXAMINER'S TIP: WRITING ABOUT THE NOVEL'S THEMES 🔓

The repetition of **themes** is often an indicator of messages the writer is trying to convey. The children and Boo have shown great courage. Societal prejudice is again referred to, in relation to Boo and Bob Ewell. The mockingbird theme is re-emphasised.

The end of the text is also a good place to look for a summary of the writer's point of view. Atticus's final words about most people being nice when you finally see them reiterates the key lesson that Scout has finally learnt: 'you never really know a man until you stand in his shoes and walk around in them' (Chapter 31, p. 285).

Everything is concluded: Scout has seen Boo, Bob Ewell is dead and justice has been done. When Scout says, 'there wasn't much else left for us to learn' (Chapter 31, p. 286), we are reminded of the **genre** (**bildungsroman**) and of the fact that Scout's formative years will soon come to an end. The teaching she has received will stand her in good stead.

However, Scout still has a few years to go until she is able to look back as a more mature **narrator**.

CHECKPOINT 15

Has the reader been prepared by earlier incidents for Boo to save the children?

KEY QUOTE

Scout's words are poignant and show great maturity when she says that if the incident was exposed to the public 'it'd be sort of like shootin' a mocking-bird' (Chapter 30, p. 282).

GLOSSARY

The Grey Ghost a book referred to right at the start of the novel; its reappearance could be to achieve a sense of a completed circle and to remind us how the children felt about the 'ghost' of Boo at the beginning

---

Progress and revision check

REVISION ACTIVITY

❶ What are the names of the two families Scout tells Miss Caroline Fisher about at school who feature later on in the novel? (Write your answers below)

....

❷ Whose house burns down?

....

❸ Why does Jem have to read to Mrs Dubose for a month?

....

❹ Who are the key participants in the trial?

....

❺ What happens to Jem when he is attacked after the Halloween pageant?

....

REVISION ACTIVITY

On a piece of paper write down answers to these questions:

● When Mr Gilmer says to Tom Robinson '*You* felt sorry for *her*, you felt *sorry* for her?' why does this spell doom for Tom?

Start: *When Tom Robinson shows sympathy for Mayella Ewell he is breaking a social code i.e., a black man showing sympathy for a white woman ...*

● Why does Boo Radley stay inside his house all the time?

Start: *Originally Boo stayed in his house as a punishment ...*

GRADE BOOSTER ★

Answer this longer, practice question about the plot/action of the novel:

Q: In what ways does the children's story of Part One prepare us for the trial episodes of Part Two?

For a C grade: Describe how key characters are introduced and described in Part One, the Maycomb setting is established, and how social and historical context prepares us for the racial prejudice of the jury in the trial in Part Two. Use textual detail to support your views.

For an A grade: Make sure you do all the above, as well as carefully selecting quotations which you use confidently and persuasively to back up your evidence. Your knowledge and use of literary terms will show your understanding of what the author is trying to achieve. Make sure you refer to the wider context of prejudice when the novel was set, and how readers past and present will be affected by this. Use your own ideas as this will impress the examiner.

PART THREE: Characters

Atticus

WHO IS ATTICUS?

Atticus, the single parent of Jem and Scout, is Maycomb's lawyer and conscience, who defends a black man accused of rape.

WHAT DOES ATTICUS DO IN THE NOVEL?

- Atticus teaches his children important lessons such as understanding other people's viewpoints (Chapter 3).
- Atticus shoots a mad dog to protect the community (Chapter 10).
- Atticus sits outside the Maycomb jail to protect Tom Robinson from a lynch mob (Chapter 15).
- Atticus defends Tom Robinson, a black man accused of raping a white woman (Chapters 17–21).
- Atticus agrees to keep quiet about the details of the incident with Bob Ewell (Chapter 30).

HOW IS ATTICUS DESCRIBED AND WHAT DOES IT MEAN?

Quotation	Means?
'we were ... free to interrupt Atticus for a translation'	Atticus uses formal language but is patient and happy to explain things. He believes in being honest, respectful and straightforward with his children.
'Atticus Finch is the same in his house as he is on the public streets.'	Atticus is always consistent and courteous. This is usually a good thing, but his ideals and principles can put him and his family at risk in society.
'He sat in the living-room and read.'	He is a studious lawyer, not young and active. He does not conform to society's view of what it is to be a Southern gentleman and is something of a loner.
'he's the only man in these parts who can keep a jury out so long.'	A persuasive lawyer, he is determined that Tom Robinson gets a fair trial. Racial prejudice means he can't win, but he will try to change things.

EXAMINER'S TIP: WRITING ABOUT ATTICUS

Make sure you not only discuss what Atticus does, such as teaching the children important lessons and defending Tom Robinson, but also how he does this, and what his actions are displaying. You could see him as Harper Lee's spokesman, embodying the themes of justice, tolerance, goodness and courage. Yet despite his strong principles and idealism, he is trapped within the society in which he lives.

DID YOU KNOW

It is significant that Atticus Finch was named after a Roman who refused to join either side in the Civil War (109–32 BC). In ancient times, there was also a philosopher called Atticus, who was well known for his kindly **character** and for his love of truth.

DID YOU KNOW

Atticus's style of parenting was probably quite forward-thinking at the time and his way of dealing with his children sometimes clashed with other adults in the story.

KEY CONNECTIONS

See if you can get hold of the 1962 film version of the novel. Do you think Gregory Peck was a good choice of actor to play Atticus?

Scout

WHO IS SCOUT?

The **narrator** of the novel, Scout tells the story of her childhood, giving us her perspective on the Tom Robinson trial and other events.

WHAT DOES SCOUT DO IN THE NOVEL?

- Scout starts school for the first time (Chapter 2).

- Scout discovers gifts hidden in a tree near the Radley house (Chapter 4).

- Scout finds her father outside the Maycomb jail and helps bring to an end a dangerous situation (Chapter 15).

- Scout is present at the trial of Tom Robinson (Chapters 17–21).

- Scout attends a Maycomb Missionary Society meeting (Chapter 24).

- Scout performs in the Halloween pageant and is attacked on her way home (Chapters 28–9).

HOW IS SCOUT DESCRIBED AND WHAT DOES IT MEAN?

Quotation	Means?
'she discovered that I was literate and looked at me with more than faint distaste'	Scout's teacher does not approve of Scout's advanced reading skills, but Scout, a bright, unconventional child, has grown up in a household full of newspapers and books.
'You're also growing out of your pants a little'	Uncle Jack is referring both to Scout's cheeky behaviour and to her tomboy nature. She rarely wears dresses, which she learns will get in the way of her becoming a 'lady'.
'when you ... are grown, maybe you'll look back on this with some compassion and some feeling that I didn't let you down'	Through the two perspectives of the child and adult Scout, we see that the narrator supports, and even idealises Atticus, despite his limitations.
'there wasn't much else left for us to learn, except possibly algebra'	Scout's words are an indication of her precociousness and also of how much she's been through. Her character has been strengthened, rather than altered, by her recent experiences.

EXAMINER'S TIP: WRITING ABOUT SCOUT

You should both describe Scout's personality and consider why she has these characteristics. For instance, it is through Scout's sociable nature that the reader encounters a variety of characters and situations. Bright and articulate, she can absorb what is going on and give a full picture of the action. Her naivety provides an opportunity for humour and **irony**.

You will impress the examiner if you not only back up your arguments to show Scout's development, contrasting her behaviour at the novel's beginning and end, but also point out that the mature narrator is not a character we get to know well. We do discover, however, that the grown-up Scout is intelligent, creative and informative about history, literature and Southern ways (like Harper Lee?).

Jem

Jem is Scout's brother and constant companion. Four years older than Scout, she clearly looks up to him, as we see from such comments as, 'In all his life, Jem had never declined a dare' (Chapter 1, p. 19).

He is generally a sensible, rational and intelligent boy. On the occasion when Jem behaves out of character, cutting off Mrs Dubose's camellias (Chapter 11), he learns his biggest lesson about courage.

As Jem is going through a period of physical and mental change, his mood and behaviour at times reflect this.

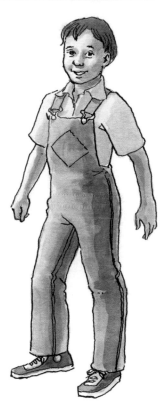

> **KEY QUOTE**
>
> Scout: 'He was difficult to live with, inconsistent, moody' (Chapter 12, p. 121).

> **KEY QUOTE**
>
> Scout: 'Jem was becoming almost as good as Atticus at making you feel right when things went wrong' (Chapter 28, p. 265).

- Jem is a natural leader. His creative and resourceful nature is brought out in the games he plays with Dill and Scout.

- Jem is idealistic and thoughtful, and, in contrast to Scout, we see that he takes it very much to heart when Tom Robinson is declared guilty as he has a strong sense of justice.

- Jem's maturity is charted in the novel, for instance when he tells Atticus about Dill having run away.

- Jem is a mirror of Atticus, even in his ambition to become a lawyer to bring about change.

- In Jem, Harper Lee seems to imply that what has not been achieved by Atticus may later be achieved by Jem – reassuring us that there will be people like Atticus in the future.

Calpurnia (Cal)

Calpurnia is the Finch family cook, but she also plays a big part in bringing up and educating Scout and Jem. She has gained Atticus's respect as a 'faithful member' (Chapter 14, p. 142) of the family. She is strict with the children, but also has a sense of compassion and is kind to them when they are finding life difficult.

- Calpurnia represents the bridge between the white and black communities.

- Calpurnia gives Atticus and the children information about the Robinson family.

- Calpurnia takes Scout and Jem to the black community church, thus providing the children with valuable information that will inform them during the trial.

- Atticus uses Calpurnia to thank the black community for their gifts to him after the trial, but reminds her to tell them that they mustn't do this again as life is hard.

- Calpurnia is the person that Atticus chooses to accompany him to tell Helen Robinson of her husband's death.

Dill (Charles Baker Harris)

Dill comes from Mississippi every summer to stay with his aunt, Rachel Haverford, and to play with Jem and Scout who live next door. He features largely in the first part of the novel where he is fascinated with Boo Radley, and goads Jem and Scout into trying to see this mystery figure. In the second part of the novel Dill is only present as a contrast to Jem and Scout – we do not see his **character** mature as we do with the others.

As Dill is only a Maycomb inhabitant during the summer, he can be used to provide information to the reader at key moments in the novel when Scout or Jem fill him in.

- Dill's family background is very different from that of Scout and Jem. His father seems to have little contact with him and his family show little concern for his well-being.

- At the trial, Harper Lee contrasts Dill's sensitive nature with the logical and rational Jem.

- Whereas Jem wants to confront prejudice, Dill decides to accept things the way they are and make the best of them – consequently his choice of profession will be a laughing clown!

- Dill has a curious and quick-thinking nature.

- Dill dwells in his 'own twilight world' (Chapter 14, pp. 149–50) and gives the impression that his wild imagination is stimulated by unhappiness in his life.

Tom Robinson

The character of Tom Robinson, like Boo Radley, is not explored in great depth. However, a large proportion of Part Two is concerned with Tom's story, and he is crucial in developing the overall **themes** and **symbols** of the novel. Both he and Boo, it can be argued, are the mockingbirds of the novel.

We see from scenes such as the one with the Missionary Society women that at the time when this novel was set, that black people were not always seen as fully rounded people. Any negative traits, like the anger of the black community following the trial for instance, seem to be seized upon by the white community. Perhaps Harper Lee was aware of such attitudes in wider society and therefore made a conscious effort to focus on the good in the black characters in her novel.

- Tom is married to Helen and they have three children. The family is part of the respectable, church-going black community.

- Tom is revealed as polite and honourable in court, where he was shown to be happy to help Mayella for no payment. His manners, according to Scout, 'were as good as Atticus's' (Chapter 19, p. 201).

- Tom's perception of Mayella's loneliness and need, however, gets him into trouble.

- Atticus proves Tom's innocence by drawing attention to his weakened left arm. However, as a symbol of the black community (see **Key theme: Prejudice**) Tom is found guilty.

- In despair, Tom tries to escape from jail and is shot in cold blood.

> **KEY QUOTE**
>
> Atticus concludes, 'I guess Tom was tired of white men's chances and preferred to take his own' (Chapter 24, p. 242).

Boo (Arthur) Radley

Boo Radley is a largely mysterious figure who is mocked by the wider community, as well as by Jem, Scout and Dill as they become fascinated by this man who never leaves the house. His character gradually emerges and it is not until the end of the novel that he is 'seen' by Scout, both physically and **metaphorically**, when he heroically rescues Jem from Bob Ewell. His childhood misdemeanours have led to a lifetime's imprisonment by Mr and Mrs Radley and his older brother Nathan.

- Boo becomes the focus of Scout, Jem and Dill's childhood games, as they try to catch a glimpse of him.

- Boo leaves gifts for the children.

- Boo wraps a blanket around Scout's shoulders during the fire.

- Boo emerges as a lonely, kind figure, harmlessly watching over Scout's and Jem's lives.

- After she is rescued by him, Scout recognises that exposing Boo to the public would be 'sort of like shootin' a mocking-bird' (Chapter 30, p. 282).

> **KEY QUOTE**
>
> Boo in Chapter 1 is described by Jem as 'six-and-a-half feet tall', eating 'raw squirrels and any cats he could catch'; his 'hands were blood-stained', and he had a 'long jagged scar' and eyes that 'popped' (p. 19). Notice the realistic description of Boo at the end of Chapter 29.

Aunt Alexandra

Alexandra Finch is Atticus and Uncle Jack's sister, Jem and Scout's aunt, Francis's grandmother. She lives at Finch's Landing, which is associated with a past of cotton-growing and slave-owning. Unlike her brothers, she has not moved away and made a new life for herself and perhaps consequently, as Scout discovers, she holds onto traditional views and is obsessed with family heredity. Although Aunt Alexandra is not favourably portrayed by Scout, she has several redeeming moments, and these give a more rounded picture than if her character had remained the same throughout.

- Aunt Alexandra first features in the story when Atticus, Jem and Scout go to spend Christmas at Finch's Landing.

- Aunt Alexandra disapproves of Scout's tomboy ways. She is very concerned with turning her niece into a 'lady', and thus provides a contrast to other main adult characters like Atticus and Miss Maudie.

- Aunt Alexandra becomes a major character in the plot when she invites herself to stay at the Finch home to help Atticus with the children during the difficult trial period.

- Aunt Alexandra and Atticus have fundamentally different attitudes to child rearing and servant supervision, Aunt Alexandra displaying prejudiced behaviour and applying strict rules of conduct.

- When Aunt Alexandra expresses sympathy for Atticus at the news of Tom Robinson's death, detaching herself from the hypocritical Missionary Society meeting, Scout is suddenly able to appreciate the dignity of her aunt's behaviour.

> **KEY QUOTE**
>
> Scout comments on her aunt's arrival: 'Aunt Alexandra fitted into the world of Maycomb like a hand into a glove, but never into the world of Jem and me' (Chapter 13, p. 137).

Miss Maudie Atkinson

As Scout and Jem's neighbour, who is always working in her garden, Miss Maudie is a source of information and company for the children. As with Calpurnia, the reader feels positive towards this character because Scout and Atticus like and value her. Her major role in the plot seems to be to reinforce Atticus's philosophy, and to be a constant and reassuring model for the children when Atticus is busy elsewhere.

Miss Maudie may be a mouthpiece for Harper Lee's views, as at certain times are Atticus and Scout. For instance, Miss Maudie shows her disapproval of 'foot-washers' who 'think women are a sin by definition' (Chapter 5, p. 51). She despises prejudice of any kind. This is shown by Scout's first description of her – she 'loved everything that grew in God's earth' (Chapter 5, p. 48) with the exception of nut grass, which is hugely symbolic of prejudice that can sweep through a society.

- Miss Maudie is an especially important female role model for Scout.

- After major stressful events in the novel, Miss Maudie is always there for the children to provide sensible human philosophy.

- When Miss Maudie's house burns down and she does not seem too upset at losing her largest material possession, her reaction has a big impact on the children.

- Miss Maudie disapproves of neighbourhood gossip. She dislikes how the town comes out to watch 'a poor devil on trial for his life' (Chapter 16, p. 165), and silences Mrs Merriweather over her hypocrisy at Aunt Alexandra's tea-party.

> **KEY QUOTE**
>
> Miss Maudie: 'Why, one sprig of nut-grass can ruin a whole yard ... the wind blows it all over Maycomb County!' (Chapter 5, p. 48)

Other Maycomb characters

THE EWELLS

The Ewells are a poor, ill-educated family, who represent the prejudiced element of the community. The comments about Burris Ewell at school help to build an impression of a dysfunctional and uncared for family, and Mayella Ewell is the white woman who accuses Tom Robinson of rape.

Mayella has no mother and has no help in bringing up a large family. She is shown to be lonely and neglected. This lack of love, warmth and human contact leads Mayella to grab Tom, as she wants to be kissed by a man. She is a pathetic figure at the trial.

Robert Ewell, the father, has his major scene at the trial, where he is rude, bigoted and foul-mouthed (see **Language: The language characters speak**). There is a strong indication that he abuses Mayella and that it was he who beat her up. His vicious acts of revenge against Tom, Atticus and Judge Taylor are the driving force of the final chapters.

Through Robert Ewell's death at the end, the novelist seems to be saying that he is beyond hope, or perhaps that justice must be seen to be done. Perhaps his death represents hope for the future, as the fear he caused, which created a barrier to truth and understanding, has been removed. Mayella's flowers at the Ewell residence can now begin to flourish.

THE CUNNINGHAMS

The Cunningham family is also poor, but, in contrast to the Ewells who are from the city, they are country folk, whose pride is evident from the outset, when Walter refuses to accept something he cannot repay on his first day of school. Mr Cunningham also shows this family trait by paying Atticus for his law work in ways other than money. He shows a basic goodness by dispersing the racist mob once his eyes are 'opened' by Scout.

A different member of the family, one of the jurors, has great difficulty finding Tom guilty. Harper Lee is showing that if groups of people like these can, if only for a moment, stand in another's shoes and see their viewpoint, then there has to be hope for the future.

MRS HENRY LAFAYETTE DUBOSE

Mrs Henry Lafayette Dubose is another Finch neighbour, who is known as the 'meanest old woman who ever lived' (Chapter 4, p. 41). She is an important character as Jem has to read to her after he beheads her camellia bushes, and when she dies the children learn that she was struggling to combat a morphine addiction. Atticus uses this episode to teach them a lesson on courage.

> **KEY QUOTE**
>
> Atticus: 'I wanted you to see what real courage is, instead of getting the idea that courage is a man with a gun in his hand' (Chapter 11, p. 118).

MORE MINOR CHARACTERS

Mr Heck Tate – a key witness in the trial and the town sheriff, who later takes justice into his own hands.

Judge John Taylor – the elderly judge in the Tom Robinson trial, of high moral calibre and displaying unconventional behaviour.

Mr Gilmer – the solicitor representing Mayella Ewell.

Mr Link Deas – an owner of a cotton-picking farm who offers Tom and Helen Robinson work. He speaks up for Tom out of turn in court and defends Helen Robinson against Bob Ewell.

Mr Underwood – the owner, editor and printer of *The Maycomb Tribune* who 'despises' black people (Chapter 16, p. 162), but the lynch mob incident and his article after Tom's death suggest he despises injustice even more.

Doctor Reynolds – Maycomb's doctor and Finch family friend.

Miss Caroline Fisher and Miss Gates – Scout's schoolteachers.

Little Chuck Little – a member of Scout's class, from a poor background but a 'born gentleman' (Chapter 3, p. 31).

Cecil Jacobs – Scout's classmate and neighbour, who taunts Scout with prejudice against her father. He also jumps out on Jem and Scout on their way to the pageant.

Mr Dolphus Raymond – a white man from a rich family who lives with a black woman and their children. The white community look down on him as he seems permanently drunk, but Scout and Dill learn that by pretending to drink he is giving the white community a 'reason' for his chosen way of life.

Zeebo – Calpurnia's son. He reads hymns at the black community church and is the local rubbish collector.

Lula May – a black woman who objects to Scout and Jem being at the black community church.

Reverend Sykes – the leader of the black community church. He finds seats for Jem, Scout and Dill at the trial and offers his view of events.

Miss Stephanie Crawford – a Finch neighbour, concerned with triviality and local gossip.

Mrs Grace Merriweather – a prominent, devout figure of the Maycomb Missionary Circle and organiser of the pageant.

Misses Tutti and Frutti Barber – Maycomb sisters who are old and deaf.

CHECKPOINT 16

In what general ways could Mrs Merriweather be likened to Harper Lee?

Progress and revision check

REVISION ACTIVITY

❶ Who says 'You never really understand a person until you consider things from his point of view – until you climb into his skin and walk around in it'? (Write your answers below)

....

❷ Which of Jem and Scout's neighbours does this describe: 'She had never told on us ... she was not at all interested in our private lives'?

....

❸ Which character in the trial scenes is described as 'the loneliest person in the world' and why is she lonely?

....

❹ Which characters appear to speak for Harper Lee?

....

❺ Who is this said about: 'This is their home, sister ... We've made it this way for them, they might as well learn to cope with it'?

....

REVISION ACTIVITY

On a piece of paper write down answers to these questions:

● Who do we learn more about in the novel: Tom or Calpurnia?

Start: *Although Part Two is largely concerned with Tom's story, we never fully get to know Tom Robinson, unlike Calpurnia, who is more real to the reader as we see her interact with other characters ...*

● At what stage does Jem begin to enter his adolescent phase?

Start: *At the beginning of Part Two, we learn that Jem is growing up ...*

GRADE BOOSTER ★

Answer this longer, practice question about the characters of the novel:

Q: In what ways does Harper Lee show how the children's view of Boo Radley changes throughout the novel?

For a C grade: Explain how the writer presents Boo at the beginning of the novel, and what the children's games tell us about what they think about Boo. Find as many details as you can where Boo is mentioned indirectly. Describe Boo's appearance at the end of the novel, and how his physical description and character seem very different from his earlier imagined persona. Use short quotations and specific examples in the text to back up your argument.

For an A grade: Make sure you do all of the above, as well as using quotations confidently within your argument. As well as describing the events which lead to a change in the children's view, discuss how other incidents, for instance that of the trial, give the children a wider view of prejudice, and sympathy, thus informing a change in their view of Boo. You may also refer to characters like Dolphus Raymond and Aunt Alexandra, and how the children's viewpoint changes towards them too. Use your opinions confidently to back up your views.

PART FOUR: KEY CONTEXTS AND THEMES

 **DID YOU KNOW**

Harper Lee gave all three of her mother's names to characters in the novel – emphasising its **auto-biographical** nature. She has admitted, too, that Atticus is largely based on her father, also a lawyer.

KEY CONNECTIONS

Hugh Brogan's *Penguin History of the United States of America* (1990) contains useful background information, for instance on the Economic Depression, which is relevant to this novel.

 **DID YOU KNOW**

All the young men accused, except for the youngest who was aged twelve, were sentenced to death after several trials (1931–6).

Key contexts

THE AUTHOR

Nelle Harper Lee (known as Harper Lee) was born in Monroeville on 28 April 1926. Her parents were Amasa Coleman Lee and Frances Cunningham Finch Lee. The writer Truman Capote was also brought up in Monroeville and was a childhood friend of Harper Lee.

In the 1930s and 1940s Harper Lee attended local schools in Monroeville, before moving to Montgomery, Alabama, aged eighteen, to study. However, she gave up her law studies at the University of Alabama to move to New York to become a writer, and in 1960 finally published *To Kill a Mockingbird*, her first and only novel. It immediately won critical acclaim – and is still a bestselling classic today.

THE ECONOMIC DEPRESSION 1933–5

Following the Wall Street Crash in 1929, America's Great Economic Depression began and poverty swept the country. President Roosevelt made substantial attempts at economic recovery. After the National Recovery Act, Roosevelt told the people 'they had nothing to fear but fear itself'. However, it took time to relieve people's suffering and hardship.

We see the consequences of this poverty in Maycomb. We are told that the Cunninghams are from the countryside, and the Crash had hit these people hardest. The difficulties are also referred to at other times, such as when black people bring gifts following the trial and Atticus tells Calpurnia that they shouldn't as 'Times are too hard' (Chapter 22, p. 220).

THE CIVIL WAR AND THE CIVIL RIGHTS MOVEMENT

The abolition of slavery after the American Civil War of 1861–5 changed the legal position of black people in American society. White people now saw black people as potential competitors for jobs, particularly in the hard years of the Economic Depression during which *To Kill a Mockingbird* is set. Fear and paranoia led to the 'white' belief that black people desired all that white people had, including marrying white women.

In the 1930s when Harper Lee was a child the Scottsboro trials in Alabama found nine black young men guilty of raping two white women. Some time later it was discovered they were all innocent.

In the 1950s while Harper Lee was writing her novel, the Civil Rights Movement was getting under way, with black people calling for desegregation and starting to demand more civil rights, such as the right to vote. Alabama, where Martin Luther King was based, was an important centre in the Movement.

These historic events led to Harper Lee's novel, which is a mixture of nostalgia, criticism and perhaps guilt – typical of white writers in the American South at the time who had gained some perspective on the isolated communities in which they grew up.

SETTING AND PLACE

Maycomb is a microcosm of American society in the 1930s, especially that of the Southern States.

With the background of economic hardship and racial prejudice, as well as the historical impact of the Civil War, we see how the geographical setting has a direct impact on shaping both the **characters** and the plot of *To Kill a Mockingbird.*

EXAMINER'S TIP: WRITING ABOUT CULTURE, SETTING AND PLACE

Knowledge of where the novel is located in a historical and geographical sense, and learning about the culture of the American South in the 1930s, will give you a far better understanding of the events that take place.

The examiner wants to see not only references to the novel's background, but also how it affected its **themes** and influential characters.

Try the following:

- Consider the ideal of 'Southern womanhood' and women as delicate, fragile creatures, and how this would have influenced the men's feelings and responsibility towards Mayella Ewell during the trial.

- Think about how traditional views might make a community wary of 'different' people, such as the Radleys.

If you can display such knowledge and carefully link it with the novel's themes, you will impress the examiner – especially if you quote directly from the text, and even refer to your own modern perspective.

DID YOU KNOW

All sections of society were hit by the Great Depression, because, as Atticus explains to Scout, professionals like doctors and lawyers depended on farmers for their income but they had no money and therefore had to pay them with services and goods instead (Chapter 2, p. 27).

KEY CONNECTIONS

Truman Capote also wrote about a child growing up in the Southern States of America in roughly the same period. See *Other Voices, Other Rooms* (1948).

Key themes

GROWING UP

Scout

To Kill a Mockingbird shows Scout's growing awareness of the world around her. The story is told by a mature **narrator** who is looking back at her past. Scout's naivety is highlighted when the reader understands events better than Scout herself.

Over the course of the novel Scout learns various lessons:

- From **Calpurnia**: politeness should be shown to all people (Chapter 3).
- From **Atticus**: to be tolerant, to react calmly to events (Chapter 9), to be able to turn the other cheek, to appreciate different kinds of courage (Chapters 10 and 11).
- From **Aunt Alexandra**: the value of being a 'lady' (Chapter 24).
- From **Heck Tate and Atticus**: the destructive implications of society's prejudice (from the trial onwards), even if Scout has not yet been able to appreciate fully why prejudice exists.

By the end of the novel Scout has successfully learnt Atticus's key lesson – that of seeing another person's point of view. We witness a dramatic transformation in her behaviour towards Boo. She is still a child, however, and after her traumatic incident with Bob Ewell she returns to *The Grey Ghost*, a book she was reading at the beginning of the novel. She feels she has learnt all she can for the moment.

Jem

At the beginning of the novel Jem likes to play superstitious games about Boo Radley with Scout and Dill. The start of Jem's maturing is marked when:

- He goes to retrieve his trousers (Chapter 6).
- He organises the building of the snowman – not seeing this as a game, but taking a mature approach to finding resources (Chapter 8).
- He begins to recognise Boo's human side (Chapter 8) and the childish games end.

Jem gradually becomes more separate from Scout and Dill, particularly after his punishment involving Mrs Dubose (Chapter 11). His transition from childhood to adulthood is acknowledged in different ways: Miss Maudie gives him a slice from the big cake (Chapter 22) and Calpurnia starts calling him 'Mister Jem' (Chapter 12). Instead of encouraging Scout to be a tomboy, he now tells her she should start behaving like a girl. He takes a mature approach by telling Atticus that Dill has run away from home. Jem is proud of his first signs of physical maturity (Chapter 23) and shows an emotional response to the injustices of the trial (Chapters 22–3). Although not a young child any more, he is having trouble coming to terms with the adult world.

By the end of the novel Jem has taken on some adult attitudes and views. He has learnt from Atticus's example – for instance, when he tries to make Scout feel better about her mistake after the pageant (Chapter 28).

KEY CONNECTIONS

Mildred Taylor's *Roll of Thunder, Hear My Cry* (1976) has many of the same **themes**. It is told by a black girl narrator and set in the 1930s in the American South. Compare and contrast.

EXAMINER'S TIP

All of Scout's educational experiences and growing up take place outside school. Charles Dickens's *Hard Times* (1854) similarly depicts an education system irrelevant to the children's everyday existence. Referring to other works of literature may impress the examiner.

EXAMINER'S TIP: WRITING ABOUT THE CHILDREN GROWING UP

Make sure that, as well as referring to some of the specific incidents of the children's growth with short quotations to back up your argument, you point out that Jem's growing up is easier to chart than Scout's because:

- It is easier to report about another character than to record what is happening to oneself.

- Jem's age means that he bridges two distinct periods, from childhood to adolescence. Thus his growing up is more radical, and is more obvious when contrasted with Scout's.

Discuss what Jem may be like as a man. Will he have some of Atticus's characteristics?

Does the author show sadness about the children growing up? Consider, for example, Harper Lee's **epigraph** and when Atticus says to Jem in Chapter 23: 'So far nothing in your life has interfered with your reasoning process' (p. 226).

REVISION ACTIVITY

It would be difficult to find just three or four examples where the **theme** of growing up is most prominent in the novel, as Jem and Scout undergo a gradual process of growth. Discovering that Boo is a person with real feelings (e.g. finding presents in the knot-hole) and learning about prejudice during the trial are arguably the two major times when the children grow up. However, when re-reading the novel, make a note of separate incidents that show Jem and Scout growing up, as these specific examples will strengthen your argument.

PREJUDICE

Prejudice is arguably the most prominent theme of the novel. It is directed towards groups and individuals in the Maycomb community and linked with ideas of fear, superstition and injustice. The dominant form of prejudice in the novel is racial prejudice. The period during which Harper Lee was writing and the time at which the novel was set would have greatly informed her presentation of this topic.

Maycomb is divided into clearly defined groups. The black community in Maycomb is automatically seen as the bottom of the social strata, below the lowest class of white people – the Ewells – who are categorised by the community as 'White Trash'. When Tom shows that he felt sorry for Mayella this is immediately seized upon by Mr Gilmer, as it would be interpreted as the lowest class of citizen showing superiority towards a class above it. The Ewells would have felt very threatened by the black community as, after the abolition of slavery, there was no longer a clear distinction between the white lower class and the black community.

DID YOU KNOW

Although the trial is mainly an issue of racial prejudice, we see that the lynch mob (Chapter 15) is so hateful that it even tries to prevent Tom gaining a court hearing – the most basic form of justice. Class and gender prejudice also contributed to the unjust verdict of guilty.

DID YOU KNOW

Jem recognises the class structure when he talks of 'four kinds of folks in the world' (Chapter 23, p. 232); Aunt Alexandra claims that every family had a particular 'Streak' (Chapter 13, p. 135); and Scout documents the 'caste system' (Chapter 13, p. 137), in which very particular family characteristics have developed.

CHECKPOINT 17

Mayella obviously had in mind the idea of Southern womanhood – that women were to be worshipped and protected – when she played on the white men's conscience at the trial. How did she do this?

? DID YOU KNOW

We have to be reminded that in 1930s America women couldn't vote, and lacked many of the basic rights accorded to men.

CHECKPOINT 18

Try to find as many examples as possible of where Atticus's maxim is stated.

GRADE BOOSTER

If you take note of any other small examples of prejudice and weave these into your essays, this may improve your grade – especially if you find examples that are not the most obvious ones.

Although women are not seen as a separate class group, we learn – from Miss Maudie in terms of religion (Chapter 5) and from Atticus in terms of the law – that women are regarded as unequal to men by the Maycomb community. They are not permitted to sit on the jury (Chapter 23) and Scout learns that women are expected to behave and dress in a certain way. When Atticus says about Tom's trial that he is 'in favour of Southern womanhood as much as anybody, but not for preserving polite fiction at the expense of human life' (Chapter 15, p.153), we see how entrenched this idealised view of women is.

Harper Lee broadens discussion of the topic of prejudice, showing how different kinds are interlinked. She indicates that the unstable economic situation and isolated nature of the community means that prejudice is directed towards all sorts of **characters** who do not fit into the expected behavioural patterns of society. One example is the Radley family. Another is Miss Caroline Fisher, who is from North Alabama and thus considered a kind of foreigner.

Atticus's **maxim** – that if you attempt to stand in another's shoes you will be able to see their point of view – leads to understanding and tolerance rather than prejudice. For instance, when the children realise that Boo is a real person prejudice towards him dies. Atticus repeats and demonstrates this lesson to the children, such as when he tries to sympathise with Mrs Dubose and Bob Ewell. At the trial he attempts to get the white jury to stand in Tom Robinson's shoes. We see that Scout and Jem learn to do this with various characters, such as when Scout sympathises with Mayella Ewell's loneliness at the trial.

Atticus's response to Scout, saying Boo was 'real nice' right at the end of the novel (Chapter 31, p. 287), leaves the reader on an upbeat note: 'Most people are, Scout, when you finally see them' (Chapter 31, p. 287). This implies that although those barriers of prejudice have not yet broken down, it is only a matter of time. We have to remind ourselves that we are looking back with hindsight; the novel's characters could never have envisaged an African-American becoming president of the United States!

EXAMINER'S TIP: WRITING ABOUT HARPER LEE'S VIEWS ON BREAKING DOWN PREJUDICE

It is worth citing some examples of prejudice and of how Atticus and Scout (and other characters) challenge this prejudice. A discussion of how Atticus's maxim, and the theme of the mockingbird, work through the novel would be very useful.

Harper Lee seems to indicate that the breaking down of prejudice has to be targeted towards individuals initially, like the Cunningham man at the trial. 'Baby steps' have to be taken instead of eliminating prejudice all at once. The author, for all her forward-thinking, may be considered to have the slightly patronising view that racial prejudice would only be solved when white people changed their views. In fact, it was really undertaken when black civil rights were gained – by and for black people. However, we need to make reference constantly to the fact that we now have a completely different perspective, and the benefit of hindsight.

Harper Lee's universal aim for readers of *To Kill a Mockingbird* seems to be for them to understand the lives of her characters, to live Atticus's maxim, and by doing so to appreciate similar minority characters in their own communities.

REVISION ACTIVITY

Look at these four examples where the theme of racial prejudice is prominent:

- The lynch mob scene (Chapter 15)
- The trial scenes ('This case is as simple as black and white' – Chapter 20, p. 209)
- Comments made at the Missionary Society tea-party about black people (Chapter 24)
- Attitudes to Dolphus Raymond, explained by him to the children (Chapter 20).

COURAGE

There are many examples of courage shown throughout the novel, such as:

- Little Chuck Little standing up to Burris Ewell in class (Chapter 3).
- Jem rescuing his trousers at night from the Radley Place (Chapter 6).
- Miss Maudie's optimism after her house has burnt down (Chapter 8).
- Atticus facing a mad dog (Chapter 10).
- Aunt Alexandra coming to live with the Finches at a difficult time (Chapter 13).
- Mr Link Deas speaking out for the Robinsons (Chapters 19 and 27).
- Boo Radley heroically rescuing Jem from Robert Ewell (Chapter 28).

Although there are many examples of physical and moral courage, the author mainly focuses on two major types:

❶ 'Real courage' (Chapter 11, p. 118) – when you continue with what you are doing even though you are fighting a losing battle. This is explained in depth in relation to Mrs Dubose, who Atticus said was the bravest person he had met.

❷ Fighting against evil and prejudice – understanding others is sometimes not enough; an act of bravery is demanded to try to prevent evil taking place and to override prejudice. An example of this type of courage is Mr Underwood's article about Tom Robinson's death in Chapter 25.

REVISION ACTIVITY

If you wish to consider four places in the novel where the theme of courage is very prominent, look at the following references:

- The end of Chapter 11
- The second half of Chapter 15
- Chapters 20–21
- The last few chapters of the novel

KEY CONNECTIONS

If you become interested in an aspect of the novel and read some wider opinions on it, the knowledge you gain might show in your essays. For instance, you might try *Racism in Harper Lee's To Kill a Mockingbird*, Greenhaven Press (2008).

GRADE BOOSTER

As you think about this theme in terms of the setting and political background to the story, consider whether *To Kill a Mockingbird* is a courageous novel for the time in which it was written.

? DID YOU KNOW

The novel's major plot encompasses both these main types of courage: Atticus represents Tom Robinson even though success is unlikely, making a stand against racial prejudice in the Maycomb community (see **Key theme: Prejudice**).

SYMBOLISM

The mockingbird motif

The mockingbird is the most significant **symbol** in the novel. This repeated image of an innocent creature makes it a strong **motif**. The mockingbird first appears in Chapter 10 when Atticus is telling the children how to use their shotguns: 'Shoot all the bluejays you want, if you can hit 'em, but remember it's a sin to kill a mockingbird' (p. 96). Scout is surprised to hear the nonjudgemental Atticus calling anything a sin. Miss Maudie explains to her that this is because mockingbirds are neither harmful nor destructive, and only make nice music for people to enjoy.

The mockingbird symbol is kept alive throughout the **narrative**, continually reminding us of the themes with which it is associated. For instance, it is referred to:

- After the mad dog incident (Chapter 10, p. 104) – Courage
- When waiting for the jury's verdict (Chapter 21, p. 216) – Prejudice
- In Mr Underwood's article about Tom's death (Chapter 25, p. 247) – Prejudice

At tense moments, even the mockingbird is silent. In moments of descriptive beauty the mockingbird is often alluded to, lurking somewhere in the background.

Harper Lee invites the reader to consider the word 'mockingbird' and all its associations: the children mock Boo's life as they make fun of and imitate it; Mayella accuses Atticus of mocking her; the trial is a mockery of justice. Tom Robinson is clearly associated with the symbol. The connection with Boo Radley is not made clear until Scout recognises in Chapter 30 that bringing Boo into the public gaze would be like shooting a mockingbird. Positioning the symbol that has been a motif throughout right at the end of the novel emphasises that the author is trying to make an important, positive point – that at last the value of the mockingbird has been appreciated!

EXAMINER'S TIP: WRITING ABOUT THE MOCKINGBIRD SYMBOL

Tom Robinson and Boo Radley are arguably the main mockingbirds of the novel:

- They both show kindness – Boo to the children; Tom to Mayella.
- They are both innocent – Boo of the evil persona with which he is associated; Tom of the crime of rape.
- Both are victims of prejudice (see **Key theme: Prejudice**).
- Both are imprisoned and potentially vulnerable – Boo is imprisoned in a separate world to protect him from people's prejudice and attention; Tom is imprisoned and later killed as a result of people's prejudice.

Back up your opinions with key mockingbird quotes. You will also impress the examiner if you can link other **characters** to this symbol, too. For example, it could be argued that Atticus exhibits mockingbird traits as he has sung Tom's song of truth to the people of Maycomb but has not been heard.

Other symbols

There are other examples of the author using a description to allude to something else:

- The Radley Place represents the privacy, isolation and unfriendliness of the Radley family. With its austere front and closed shutters and doors – which in Maycomb 'meant illness and cold weather' – we learn that the 'misery of that house' (Chapter 1, p. 15) began many years before the novel even begins.

- The tree beside the Radley Place represents Boo's character and his desire to communicate. The children acknowledge this in their letter to him: 'Dear Sir ... we appreciate everything which you have put into the tree for us' (Chapter 7, p. 68). When the knot-hole is closed up (Chapter 7) Boo's contact is denied, but when the children stand near the tree watching the fire (Chapter 8) contact is established again. Much later (Chapter 26) Scout notices the tree trunk swelling; soon afterwards Boo saves the children and Bob Ewell is found dead under the tree (Chapter 28).

- Scout and Jem's snowman suggests how superficial skin colour is to the essence of a human being. There is not much snow and there is a lot of mud, so the snowman is dark until Jem covers it with bits of snow he has found. It keeps changing colour and during the fire the snowman collapses altogether.

- Mrs Dubose's camellias represent the prejudices that cannot be brushed off easily. When Mrs Dubose expresses her deep-rooted prejudices through verbal attacks against Atticus, Jem's 'self-conscious rectitude' (Chapter 11, p. 108) gives way to fury. The destruction of prejudice is symbolised by Jem's act of cutting 'the tops off every camellia bush Mrs Dubose owned', leaving the ground 'littered with green buds and leaves' (Chapter 11, p. 109), which represents the idea of new, fresh attitudes now being given the chance to grow.

REVISION ACTIVITY

If you wish to look back to three places in the novel where the mockingbird symbolism is very prominent, turn to the following references:

- Chapter 10: The mockingbird's special characteristics are described

- Chapter 21: The mockingbird helps to create a certain **atmosphere**

- Chapter 30: The mockingbird is directly linked to one **character** by another

DID YOU KNOW

This is where symbolism overlaps setting. The Radley Place shows character, as does the description of the Ewell house. Mayella's red geraniums indicate a desire for a better life.

EXAMINER'S TIP

By reading the novel several more times, you might discover symbols that have not been noticed before. Discussing the more obscure symbols you find can show that you have looked at the text thoroughly and thought carefully about the possible meanings the writer is trying to put across.

Progress and revision check

REVISION ACTIVITY

❶ Who says 'it'd be sort of like shootin' a mocking-bird, wouldn't it?'? (Write your answers below)

....

❷ Who calls Jem 'Mister Jem' in Part Two of the novel?

....

❸ Name some different types of prejudice in *To Kill a Mockingbird*.

....

❹ Which characters in the novel display courage?

....

❺ What was the name of the famous rape trial which took place in Alabama in the 1930s?

....

REVISION ACTIVITY

On a piece of paper write down answers to these questions:

● How do the characters of Jem and Scout grow up over the course of the novel?

Start: *When we first meet Jem he is nearly ten and Scout is nearly six. The novel spans three years and over that period of time many things happen in their lives and they mature a great deal ...*

● Compare and contrast two places in the novel, describing what they symbolise.

Start: *The Ewell family and the black community live in settlements side by side in Maycomb, but although in close proximity their living standards and styles are very different, symbolising their levels of personal respect and pride. The Ewells 'lived behind the town garbage dump' (Chapter 17), and according to Atticus (Chapter 3) 'lived like animals'; whereas the black people's 'cabins looked neat and snug' (Chapter 17) ...*

GRADE BOOSTER ★

Answer this longer, practice question about a theme of the novel:

Q: What does Harper Lee say about courage in Chapter 11 of the novel?

For a C grade: Describe what happens carefully in this chapter, giving an explanation of why Mrs Dubose is showing courage in her acts. Include specific quotes to back up your argument. Refer to the fact that a character like Mrs Dubose would have lived through some interesting historical times, such as the Civil War, thus influencing her views.

For an A grade: Look at how Atticus explains that courage isn't what he has just displayed in the incident with the dog but the importance of seeing things through. Try linking this to any other themes (e.g. prejudice) and any instances of other characters displaying courage. Show how the language is used to present this theme, and how the structure of this chapter highlights this theme too. Does Scout's role of narrator affect our response to the presentation of this theme in this chapter?

PART FIVE: LANGUAGE AND STRUCTURE

Language

Here are some useful terms to know when writing about *To Kill a Mockingbird*, what they mean and how they appear in the novel.

Literary term	Means?	Example
Simile	When one thing is said to be like another, always containing the word 'like' or 'as' and allowing a comparison with things that are similar.	Scout uses many in her descriptions of people – e.g. Calpurnia's 'hand was wide as a bed slat and twice as hard' (Chapter 1, p. 12), an appropriate image as she is the housekeeper.
Metaphor	Something being described as something else.	Scout describes Atticus in court as going 'frog-sticking without a light' (Chapter 17, p. 183) when she thinks he is starting something without sufficient equipment to deal with it.
Personification	Figurative language (sometimes metaphor or simile) that treats ideas as if they are people, with human attributes and feelings.	The Radley house is described as 'droopy and sick' (Chapter 1, p. 21).
Malapropism *hyperbole*	Inaccurate use of a word	When Bob Ewell says he is most definitely not ambidextrous and can use 'one hand good as the other' (Chapter 17, p. 184).

CHECKPOINT 19

Find a simile in the text to describe Miss Caroline in Chapter 2 and Mrs Dubose in Chapter 11.

? DID YOU KNOW

As well as illuminating meaning, the frog metaphor also gives an idea of what it is like for a child to grow up in the American Southern States.

? DID YOU KNOW

Jem's definition of 'entailment' (Chapter 2, p. 26) is an example of malapropism, which is a common technique used by the author for creating humour. ('Entailment' is a legal process where a person has the use of land without being the owner of it.)

EXAMINER'S TIP: WRITING ABOUT NARRATIVE STYLE

Try occasionally looking beyond the text and making comparisons and contrasts with other texts in relation to **characters**, **themes** and structure. For instance, when talking about the theme of racial prejudice in *To Kill a Mockingbird*, you could discuss not only how historical context and the fact that it is a **regional novel** link it to other twentieth-century American writing, but also how aspects of its **narrative** style link it to traditional ideas of the nineteenth-century novel. Similarities are:

● Full, leisurely and **realistic** portrayal of a particular community
● Concern with the battle of good and evil
● Tragic and comic elements
● Sentimental feel, with a clear set of morals
● **Chronological** order of events (see **Structure**)

Wherever possible, give concrete examples of other works.

THE LANGUAGE CHARACTERS SPEAK

Harper Lee's ability to capture a variety of **dialects** and Southern **colloquial** expressions adds **realism** and authenticity to the novel. One example of a general Southern colloquialism is 'buying cotton' – a polite way of saying that a person does nothing.

Varieties of speech are often used to make a social comment about a **character**:

- Children's dialogue and the use of slang are notable (see Jem, Scout and Dill's conversation at the end of Chapter 1). The words that Scout in particular uses are very colourful, often including beautiful **figurative language** to describe other characters. Scout is very imaginative and descriptive. For instance, when she is describing in Chapter 9 how boring her cousin Francis is, she says: 'Talking to Francis gave me the sensation of settling slowly to the bottom of the ocean' (p. 87). The author is clearly skilled in capturing children's language, and also the humour that sometimes results from children trying to use language they do not understand. The perspective is not restricted, as Harper Lee tells her story as an adult.

- Atticus, mirroring his personality, speaks courteously, formally but straight-forwardly. His 'last-will-and-testament diction' (Chapter 3, p. 37) has become part of Jem and Scout's vocabulary. From a legal background herself, Harper Lee would also have been very comfortable with this language.

- Aunt Alexandra's language reveals her white middle-class status, and the author often contrasts particular words she uses with other characters' use of the same vocabulary, to show her prejudice. For example, compare Mr Raymond's use of the phrase 'run-of-the-mill' (Chapter 20, p. 207) with Aunt Alexandra's use of it (Chapter 13, p. 139). Note, too, Atticus's use of the word 'trash' (Chapter 23, p. 227) and see how different Aunt Alexandra's definition of this word is (Chapter 23, p. 231).

- Bob Ewell uses a crude, harsh language at the trial and refers to Mayella being raped 'screamin' like a stuck hog' (Chapter 17, p. 178). This is a grotesque **simile** and it shows what little love and respect he has for his daughter. His swear words in the trial serve to turn us against this character.

Dialect

- Mayella's dialect is as broad as Bob Ewell's, representing the uneducated white community. She takes offence at Atticus's forms of address ('ma'am' and 'Miss Mayella' – Chapter 18, pp. 187–8), his 'mocking' her, showing us that she has not been exposed to politeness and does not recognise basic social conventions. Interestingly, she is described by Scout as 'a steady-eyed cat with a twitchy tail' (Chapter 18, p. 187), which is not only a poignant visual image of Mayella, but also one carefully chosen by Harper Lee as cats hunt birds.

- Tom's dialect is also broad: 'every time I passed by yonder she'd have some little somethin' for me to do – choppin' kindlin', totin' water for her' (Chapter 19, p. 197). However, Tom's dialect is softer than Bob Ewell's. He calls Judge Taylor and Atticus 'suh' and 'Mr Finch' (Chapter 19, p. 197) and is the voice of politeness.

- Calpurnia speaks 'coloured-folks' talk' and 'white-folks' talk' (Chapter 12, p. 132). This reflects both her background and inherent ways (her grammar gets 'erratic' when she is angry), as well as her current position and the lack of education in the black community.

EXAMINER'S TIP: WRITING ABOUT CHANGES IN LANGUAGE OVER TIME

The author's use of language locates it in a certain period. Notice the changes in the language used in the 1950s when Harper Lee was writing, the language of the 1930s when the novel was set and the language used today. By pointing out some of the vocabulary that Harper Lee used which has a different meaning in today's society, you will show your sensitivity towards the language trends of the era. This is as important as knowledge of the historical background in terms of understanding the ideas and themes the author is trying to convey.

For example, the language used to describe black people has changed. Harper Lee and characters like Atticus and Calpurnia referred to black people as 'Negroes' and 'coloured men/women'. Today 'black' is a more acceptable term to describe skin colour, and descendants of 'Negroes' in America would now be referred to as 'African-Americans'.

Another noticeable change in language and meaning relates to 'coming out'. This term has taken on a specific meaning in recent years, but today's meaning and the meaning in the novel are nevertheless linked. Boo's 'coming out' involves him revealing who he is to the outside world that has condemned him; today's usage involves a person no longer hiding their homosexuality from a disapproving society. Both cases involve fear, being different, and making a bold statement by showing one's true self.

> **KEY CONNECTIONS**
>
> When watching the film adaptation (directed by Robert Mulligan, 1962) make a note of how far it deviates from the main plot of the novel. Is anything left out or added, and what is the effect of this?

DIFFERENT PURPOSES OF LANGUAGE

Harper Lee's clever use of a variety of language serves different purposes. These are:

- To create **atmosphere**
- To reveal character
- To create **symbolic** structure
- To support and enhance key themes
- To show authenticity
- To provide information
- To make a social comment
- To provide humour
- To reveal **irony**

Structure

The story follows the lives of the Finch family between 1933 and 1935. The string of events is **chronologically** arranged. It starts with Scout explaining the period she is looking back at. By the end of the novel, the story has come full circle.

The novel is divided into two parts:

- Part One (Chapters 1–11) focuses on the children's games, with Boo Radley as the driving force.
- Part Two (Chapters 12–31) is centred on the 'adults' game' of Tom Robinson's trial.

INTERNAL THEMES — COURAGE AND GROWING UP

The chapters of the novel cannot be viewed in isolation, as events have been arranged to develop ideas within the text. Repetitions and echoes, and the way chapters balance each other, make the major **themes** much sharper.

The theme of growing up and the way it is charted within the novel's structure is discussed at length in **Part Four: Key Contexts and Themes**. We also see in Part Four under **Symbolism** how careful placing of images like the mockingbird link up key themes and create a sense of coherence in the novel as a whole.

CHARACTER AND STRUCTURE

Another structural technique that Harper Lee uses is to present the reader with background information. This offers an insight into a particular way of life and later becomes significant in a different context. For instance, Burris Ewell's family life is described in Chapter 3 and is useful information when we later meet Mayella and Robert Ewell.

We also see evidence of careful structuring in an individual character's speech. Atticus plans the order of his questions at the trial as he knows this will have a particular effect on the jury. Harper Lee, with her law background, is also working her structure and order as she knows it will have a particular effect.

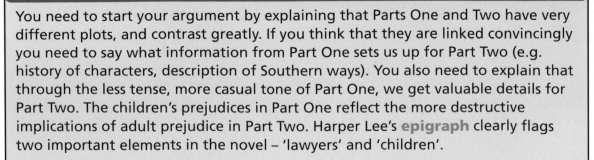

EXAMINER'S TIP: WRITING ABOUT HOW THE NARRATIVE STRUCTURE OF PART ONE SETS THE READER UP FOR PART TWO

You need to start your argument by explaining that Parts One and Two have very different plots, and contrast greatly. If you think that they are linked convincingly you need to say what information from Part One sets us up for Part Two (e.g. history of characters, description of Southern ways). You also need to explain that through the less tense, more casual tone of Part One, we get valuable details for Part Two. The children's prejudices in Part One reflect the more destructive implications of adult prejudice in Part Two. Harper Lee's **epigraph** clearly flags two important elements in the novel – 'lawyers' and 'children'.

Progress and revision check

REVISION ACTIVITY

❶ 'Jem's white shirt-tail dipped and bobbed like a small ghost dancing away to escape the coming morning' (Chapter 6, p. 63). Name the literary term used here. (Write your answers below)

....

❷ Name a character who uses very polite language.

....

❸ Who is the boy who uses impolite language to Miss Caroline in Chapter 3?

....

❹ What is the main focus of Part Two of the novel?

....

❺ Which theme is emphasised by the juxtaposition of the events involving the mad dog and Mrs Dubose (Chapters 10 and 11)?

....

REVISION ACTIVITY

On a piece of paper write down answers to these questions:

● How are themes from Part One and Part Two brought to a conclusion at the end of the novel?

Start: *When Boo Radley rescues Scout and Jem from Robert Ewell, the plots of the children's games and the trial period are finally brought together. The themes of courage, growing up, prejudice and the mockingbird symbolism are all heavily featured ...*

● How is figurative language used in the novel?

Start: *Figurative language is used by Harper Lee to lighten a story which could be seen as fairly tragic and depressing. It also helps to make the novel more realistic. Scout uses many metaphors and similes to describe characters ...*

GRADE BOOSTER

Answer this longer, practice question about the language and structure of the novel:

Q: Examine the ways narrative structure is used to convey the childish nature of the young Scout and to show the benefits of hindsight through the adult perspective.

For a C grade: Describe how the novel spans three years, and the events are told chronologically. The story takes place when the narrator (Scout) is aged nearly six to nearly nine, but she tells the story as an adult. The author carefully uses children's language, but the novel also has the coherence, knowledge and structure that only an adult could give to the story. Use specific examples as evidence, and look at how the plot is organised to show both adult and child perspectives.

For an A grade: As well as describing the techniques of the author, if you give your personal response and interpretation, and perhaps also some examples where you analyse how far the author has succeeded in this dual viewpoint, this will get you an 'A' grade. Make sure you use literary terms here to show your understanding of what Harper Lee is trying to achieve with language.

PART SIX: GRADE BOOSTER

Understanding the question

Questions in exams or controlled conditions often need **'decoding'**. Decoding the question helps to ensure that your answer will be relevant.

 UNDERSTAND EXAM LANGUAGE

Get used to exam and essay style language by looking at specimen questions and the words they use. For example:

Exam speak	Means?	Example
'convey ideas'	'get across a point to the reader' Usually you have to say how this is done.	The closed shutters of the Radley house might convey a desire for privacy.
'methods, techniques, ways'	The 'things' the writer does – such as giving a powerful description, introducing a shocking event, how someone speaks, etc.	The method of contrasting characters' speech shows politeness and rudeness e.g. Tom Robinson and Robert Ewell.
'present, represent'	1) present: 'the way in which things are told to us' 2) represent: 'what those things might mean underneath'	The writer presents the reader with descriptions of the black community's housing, representing their pride and warmth.

 'BREAK DOWN' THE QUESTION

Pick out the key words or phrases. For example:

Question: How does Harper Lee use the **character of Dolphus Raymond** to **represent** the **societal prejudice** in the novel?

- The focus is on character (Dolphus Raymond) so you will need to talk about him, what he does and how he is described by the narrator and others.
- The words **'represent the societal prejudice'** tell us that this is a question that is equally about one of the novel's themes, e.g. prejudice in Maycomb's society.

What does this tell you?

- **Focus** on Dolphus Raymond, and discuss how he is used to open a discussion about racial prejudice.

 **KNOW YOUR LITERARY LANGUAGE!**

When studying *To Kill a Mockingbird* you will come across words such as 'theme', **'symbol'**, **'imagery'**, **'simile'**, etc. Some of these words come up in the question you are asked. Make sure you know what they mean before you use them!

Planning your answer

It is vital that you **plan** your response to the controlled assessment task or possible exam question carefully, and that you then follow your plan, if you are to gain the higher grades.

 Do THE RESEARCH!

When revising for the exam, or planning your response to the controlled assessment task, collect **evidence** (for example, quotations) that will support what you have to say. For example, if preparing to answer a question on how Harper Lee has explored the theme of courage you might list ideas as follows:

Key point	Evidence/quotation	Page/chapter, etc.
Mrs Dubose displays her courage when she overcomes her morphine addiction before she dies.	Atticus says to the children, 'I wanted you to see what real courage is … It's when you know you're licked before you begin but you begin anyway and you see it through no matter what.'	Chapter 11, page 118

PLAN FOR PARAGRAPHS

Use paragraphs to plan your answer. For example:

❶ The first paragraph should **introduce** the **argument** you wish to make.

❷ Then, jot down how the paragraphs that follow will **develop** this argument. Include **details**, **examples** and other possible **points of view**. Each paragraph is likely to deal with one point at a time.

❸ **Sum up** your argument in the last paragraph.

For example, for the following task:

Question: How does Harper Lee present the character of Mayella Ewell? Comment on the language devices and techniques used.

Simple plan:

● Paragraph 1: *Introduction*

● Paragraph 2: *First point, e.g. Description of the Ewells at school before we even meet the family; Mayella's place of living described before we meet her – flowers represent her desire for a better life.*

● Paragraph 3: *Second point, e.g. Mayella's attitude in court – her unawareness of politeness, her uneducated language. Her father's attitude sheds light on this.*

● Paragraph 4: *Third point, e.g. How Tom's language and politeness contrast with this. Tom's observation of Mayella's character and situation.*

● Paragraph 5: *Fourth point, e.g. Scout's observation of Mayella's loneliness. The technique of commenting on Mayella by an outside observer.*

● Paragraph 6: *Harper Lee offers us several perspectives on Mayella Ewell, which give us a rounded understanding of her character; background of her family and home situation, and descriptions of her from Scout and other characters, help to reinforce the impression we get of Mayella when we meet her in court.*

How to use quotations

One of the secrets of success in writing essays is to use quotations **effectively**. There are five basic principles:

❶ Put quotation marks, e.g. ' ', around the quotation.
❷ Write the quotation exactly as it appears in the original.
❸ Do not use a quotation that repeats what you have just written.
❹ Use the quotation so that it fits into your sentence, or if it is longer, indent it as a separate paragraph.
❺ Only quote what is most useful.

 **USE QUOTATIONS TO DEVELOP YOUR ARGUMENT**

Quotations should be used to develop the line of thought in your essays. Your comment should not duplicate what is in your quotation. For example:

GRADE D/E	**GRADE C**
(simply repeats the idea)	(makes a point and supports it with a relevant quotation)
Miss Maudie tells Scout that her father, Atticus, is the same in his house as he is in public. She says, 'Atticus Finch is the same in his house as he is on the public streets' (Chapter 5, p. 52).	Miss Maudie indicates to Scout that her father is an honest, upfront man when she says he is the same person 'in his house as he is on the public streets' (Chapter 5, p. 52).

However, the most sophisticated way of using the writer's words is to embed them into your sentence, and further develop the point:

GRADE A

(makes point, embeds quote and develops idea)
Miss Maudie tells Scout that her father acts in an honest, consistent way when he is the same 'in his house' as he is 'on the public streets' (Chapter 5, p. 52). In this way, his professional and private personas are brought together to convey the idea of a single-minded and truthful character.

When you use quotations in this way, you are demonstrating the ability to use text as evidence to support your ideas – not simply including words from the original to prove you have read it.

EXAMINER'S TIP

Try using a quotation to begin your response. You can use it as a launch-pad for your ideas, or as an idea you are going to argue against.

Sitting the examination

Examination papers are carefully designed to give you the opportunity to do your best. Follow these handy hints for exam success:

 ## BEFORE YOU START

- Make sure that you **know the texts** you are writing about so that you are properly prepared and equipped.

- You need to be **comfortable** and **free from distractions**. Inform the invigilator if anything is off-putting, e.g. a shaky desk.

- **Read** and follow the instructions, or rubric, on the front of the examination paper. You should know by now what you need to do but **check** to reassure yourself.

- Before beginning your answer have a **skim** through the **whole paper** to make sure you don't miss anything **important**.

- Observe the **time allocation** – and follow it carefully. If they recommend 45 minutes for a particular question on a text make sure this is how long you spend.

WRITING YOUR RESPONSES

A typical 45 minute examination essay is probably between 550 and 800 words in length.

Ideally, spend a minimum of 5 minutes planning your answer before you begin.

Use the questions to structure your response. Here is an example:

Question: Do you see the ending of the novel as negative or positive? What methods does the writer use to lead you to this view?

- The introduction to your answer could briefly describe **the ending** of the novel;

- the second part could explain what could be seen as **positive**;

- the third part could be an exploration of the **negative** aspects;

- the conclusion would **sum up your own viewpoint**.

For each part allocate paragraphs to cover the points you wish to make (see **Planning your answer**).

Keep your writing clear and easy to read, using paragraphs, and link words to show the structure of your answers.

Spend a couple of minutes afterwards quickly checking for obvious errors.

'KEY WORDS' ARE THE KEY!

Keep on mentioning the **key words** from the question in your answer. This will keep you on track and remind the examiner that you are answering the question set.

> ★ **GRADE BOOSTER**
>
> Where appropriate refer to the language technique used by the writer and the effect it creates. For example, if you say, 'this **metaphor** shows how ...', or 'the effect of this metaphor is to emphasise to the reader ...' this could get you higher marks.

Sitting the controlled assessment

It may be the case that you are responding to *To Kill a Mockingbird* in a controlled assessment situation. Follow these useful tips for success.

 **KNOW WHAT YOU ARE REQUIRED TO DO**

Make sure you are clear about:

- The **specific text** and **task** you are preparing (is it just *To Kill a Mockingbird*, or more than one text?)

- How **long** you have during the assessment period (i.e. 3–4 hours?)

- How **much** you are expected or allowed to write (i.e. 2,000 words?)

- **What** you are **allowed to take** into the controlled assessment, and what you can use (or not, as the case may be!). You may be able to take in brief notes BUT NOT draft answers or detailed plans, so check with your teacher.

EXAMINER'S TIP

When discussing a theme in the novel, linking two separate pieces of action will help you to display a thorough knowledge of the text.

KNOW HOW YOU CAN PREPARE

Once you know your task, topic and text/s you can:

- Make **notes** and **prepare** the points, evidence, quotations, etc. you are likely to use.

- **Practise** or draft **model answers**.

- Use these **York Notes** to hone your **skills**, e.g. use of quotations, how to plan an answer and focus on what makes a top grade.

EXAMINER'S TIP: IN THE CONTROLLED ASSESSMENT

Remember:

- **Stick** to the **topic** and task you have been given.

- The allocated **time** is for **writing**, so make the most of it. It is **double** the time you might have in an exam, so you will be writing **almost twice** as much (or more).

- If you are allowed **access** to a dictionary or thesaurus make use of them; if not, don't go near them!

- At the end of the controlled assessment follow your teacher's **instructions**. For example, make sure you have written your name **clearly** on all the pages you hand in.

Improve your grade

It is useful to know the type of responses examiners are looking for when they award different grades. The following broad guidance should help you to improve your grade when responding to the task you are set!

GRADE C

What you need to show	What this means
Sustained response to task and text	You write enough! You don't run out of ideas after two paragraphs.
Effective use of **details** to **support** your **explanations**	You generally support what you say with evidence, e.g. Miss Caroline Fisher is naive about her new students. She doesn't understand why Walter doesn't have lunch, and reads a story unrelated to the children's lives.
Explanation of the writer's **use of language, structure, form**, etc., and the **effect on readers**	You must write about the writer's use of these things. It's not enough simply to give a viewpoint. So, you might comment on how Tom Robinson's polite language in court like 'Yes, suh' and 'No, suh' makes us feel well disposed towards him, and his embarrassment about repeating Bob Ewell's bad language makes us appreciate his honourable character.
Appropriate comment on **characters, plot, themes, ideas** and **settings**	Make sure what you say is relevant. If the task asks you to comment on the theme of prejudice, that is what you should write about.

GRADE A

What you need to show in addition to the above	What this means
Insightful, exploratory response to the text	You look beyond the obvious. You might indicate that Bob Ewell deserved to die in the end; or you might find some new aspect to comment on, e.g. he probably came from a deprived, ill-educated background and was merely replicating what he understood to be the way of things. These need not be ideas you are sure about, but you can suggest them for the examiner to consider.
Close analysis and use of **detail**	If you are looking at the writer's use of language, you comment on each word in a sentence, drawing out its distinctive effect on the reader, e.g. when Scout says 'Talking to Francis gave me the sensation of settling slowly to the bottom of the ocean', you might focus on how the word 'sensation' suggests Scout really feels physically bored by her cousin, commenting that the **simile** of 'settling slowly to the bottom of the ocean' gives a strong visual.
Convincing and **imaginative interpretation**	Your viewpoint is convincing to the examiner. You show you have engaged with the text, and come up with your own ideas. These may be based on what you have discussed in class or read about, but you have made your own decisions.

Annotated sample answers

This section will provide you with **extracts** from two **model answers**, one at **C grade** and one at **A grade**, to give you an idea of what is required to achieve at different levels.

> **Question:** Write about the parenting styles of Atticus and Robert Ewell in *To Kill a Mockingbird*.
>
> Think about:
>
> **A** Their relationships with their children and others
> **B** How Harper Lee uses language to convey these ideas

CANDIDATE 1

Could mention who Robert Ewell is too – and other comparisons

Physical description doesn't say much about parenting style

Repeats earlier quotation

Good – shows knowledge of historical background

Effective comment to apply parenting style to all readers

Atticus Finch is a lawyer, who is a widower with two young children, Jem, nearly ten years old, and Scout (the narrator), nearly six. He is helped by Calpurnia, the Finch family cook. Scout says that Atticus 'played with us, read to us, and treated us with courteous detachment' (Chapter 1).

Robert Ewell we do not meet until a little later, but when we meet Burris Ewell, one of Robert Ewell's sons, he has headlice and is rude to Miss Caroline, his teacher, showing us what Robert Ewell may be like. We learn from Atticus that none of the Ewells work and they 'lived like animals' and none of the children go to school.

Robert Ewell is introduced in the court scene as 'a little bantam cock of a man'. This is a metaphor which suggests he is like a tough, arrogant chicken. Harper Lee also reveals more about the family through Scout who talks about the family's 'filthy surroundings'. The reader learns from Robert Ewell's account that he claims relief cheques, and that he never gets a doctor out when his children are ill. These characters are living in a time of economic depression, but Harper Lee is saying that this is neglectful of his family as he spends his cheques on whisky. Tom also implies that Mayella is left to do many of the chores by herself.

Atticus works hard, but seems to be there for his children when they need him, explaining difficult ideas to them, for instance following Scout's first day of school and also after the trial. Harper Lee seems to be saying that Atticus's parenting style is the model to follow, that we should all try to learn his lessons to 'stand in' another's 'shoes and walk around in them'.

Good quotation about Atticus's parenting style

Useful quotation about the Ewells, but it doesn't say what this implies about parenting style

Refers to language use but point could be further developed, such as why it is especially apt

Could do with more on how Harper Lee uses descriptions to make comments about parenting styles

> **Overall comment:** This is a clear essay, which follows through the argument well. Perhaps some comparisons between the characters of Atticus and Robert Ewell could have been made a bit more explicitly. The student seems to run out of ideas a little, and although arguments are backed up there could be more relevant quotations and also a little more in-depth reference to the text and comment on the language and its effect.

GRADE C

CANDIDATE 2

Good to mention setting

Useful quotations backing up main body of argument

Focuses on topic and where the student plans to go

Apt to relate to second part of question

Great – referring to character's language. Would have been nice to say more about Atticus's too

Good to continually focus on Harper Lee's comments – and original point!

Atticus Finch and Robert Ewell are both widowed fathers who live in Maycomb, Alabama, in the economic hardships of the 1930s. Because they are so different, Harper Lee can make some important comparisons between their parenting styles.

Robert Ewell's family life is not presented favourably. Burris, 'the filthiest human' Scout has ever seen (Chapter 3), is rude to the teacher, and it is clear that the Ewell children are not forced to go to school, unlike Jem and Scout who 'must obey the law' (Chapter 3), a statement that re-emphasises the importance of law, and therefore Atticus, as the role model in his children's lives.

Atticus teaches several lessons to his children, such as 'You never really understand a person until you consider things from his point of view' (Chapter 3). This lesson is repeated in different contexts and Harper Lee seems to be implying that children will learn from their parents in this way, as this maxim is passed down to them.

In contrast, Harper Lee presents Ewell as 'a little bantam cock of a man', a metaphor that implies he is arrogant and ignorant, and which may explain his lack of concern for his children. For example, he doesn't call for a doctor for Mayella because of the cost. In contrast, when Jem is attacked Dr Reynolds is called immediately. Atticus is always present and consistent. Ewell seems untrustworthy and sexual abuse is hinted at. The language Ewell uses, too, shows he has no respect for his daughter, explaining that he found her 'screamin' like a stuck hog' (Chapter 17), an appropriate, if horrible, image for a rural community.

Robert Ewell's parenting style is sad, Harper Lee implies, because a child who is not properly cared for does not learn to respect others. The author seems to suggest that bad parenting can have devastating consequences, whereas effective fatherhood provides a strong role model.

Atticus aims to help not only his children see things in a new light, but all of Maycomb – and perhaps Harper Lee wants the reader to do this too!

Overall comment: This is excellent, showing analysis and original thought. Effective comparisons are made in the essay and reveal how Harper Lee uses description to comment on the two parenting styles. There could be a little more about the men's social class and background or the historical setting, but the points are supported by appropriate, embedded quotations.

GRADE A

Further questions

EXAM-STYLE QUESTIONS

❶ Prejudice is an important theme in *To Kill a Mockingbird*. What does the author say about prejudice and what methods does she use to present her ideas to the reader?

❷ Read the following extract: 'But when he noticed us dragging around the neighbourhood, not eating, taking little interest in our normal pursuits, Atticus discovered how deeply frightened we were ... he said, "What's bothering you, son?"' (Chapter 23, p. 224). Write about how Harper Lee presents Atticus and Jem in this passage. What does it say about their relationship?

❸ Look at how Harper Lee portrays Tom Robinson in the trial scenes. How does the author encourage the reader both to admire and to pity Tom? Support your answer with details from the text.

❹ Read the passage from 'The back of the Radley house was less inviting than the front ...' to 'He ran to the oak tree in his shorts.' (Chapter 6, pp. 58–60). How does Harper Lee create mood and atmosphere here?

❺ How do you respond to Aunt Alexandra in the novel? Write about:

- What Aunt Alexandra says and does that makes you respond in the way you do.

- How Harper Lee evokes the reader's response to this character through the methods she uses to write about her.

CONTROLLED ASSESSMENT-STYLE QUESTIONS

Themes and ideas

❻ *Explore the importance of a novel's setting*

Write about the importance of Maycomb as the novel's setting and how it influences key ideas and allows for key themes to be developed.

❼ *Explore the effect of a title on the way we read a novel*

Write about the title '*To Kill a Mockingbird*' and why the writer may have chosen it, in the light of the key themes and ideas in the text.

Characterisation and voice

❽ *Write about a key relationship that develops over the course of a novel you have read*

How does the writer present the characters of Jem and Scout and their relationship as they grow up over the course of the novel?

❾ *Explore the ways a novelist conveys the voice of his/her central character*

How does Harper Lee use Scout's voice to tell the story, and what techniques does she use to bring her to life?

Literary terms

Literary term	Explanation
autobiography	the story of the author's life
atmosphere	a mood or feeling
bildungsroman	a novel that describes a character's development from childhood to maturity, focusing on their experience, education and identity
character(s)	either a person in a play, novel, etc., or his or her personality
chronological	when the events in a story are told in the order they happened. It is possible to have a chronological **narrative** containing **flashbacks** as long as the main narrative continues to move forwards through time
colloquial	the everyday speech used by people in ordinary situations
dialect	accent and vocabulary, varying by region and social background
epigraph	a heading or quotation that writers sometimes use at the beginning of their work as an indication of theme
figurative language	elaborate (as distinct from plain) language. Commonly **metaphor** and **simile**
first-person narrative	stories told by an 'I' figure who is directly involved. This contrasts with the 'omniscient narrator' where the storyteller knows all and stands outside the story
flashback	a sudden jumping back to an earlier point in the **narrative** (see 'echoing' in **foreshadowing**)
foreshadowing	close to the idea of prophesying, an instance or reference to an incident coming later in the text. A contrast to 'echoing' (looking backwards)
genre	a type of literature, for instance poetry, drama, biography, fiction
imagery	descriptive language that uses images to make actions, objects and characters more vivid in the reader's mind. **Metaphors** and **similes** are examples of imagery
irony	when someone deliberately says one thing when they mean another, usually in a humorous or sarcastic way
leitmotif	see **motif**
malapropism	confused, amusing, inaccurate use of long words, so called after Mrs Malaprop in Sheridan's play *The Rivals* (1775), who refers to another character as 'the very pineapple of politeness' instead of pinnacle (malaprop from the French phrase *mal* – English equivalent, inappropriate)
maxim	a short, pithy statement proposing model human behaviour
metaphor	when one thing is used to describe another thing to create a striking or unusual image

Literary term	Explanation
motif	a repeated theme or idea. **Leitmotif** is a repeated phrase
narrative	a story or tale and the particular way that it is told. **First-person narratives** ('I') are told from the character's perspective and usually require the reader to judge carefully what is being said
narrator	(**narration**) the voice telling the story or relating a sequence of events
personification	when things or ideas are treated as if they were people, with human attributes and feelings
realism	an 'accurate' description of things as they 'really' are in 'ordinary' life
regional novel	an emphasis on particular geographical customs and speech which have a significant effect on the development of the novel
satire	aggressive **irony**. A humorous attack on human or institutional imperfection. Characterised by a ridiculing of the morally doubtful or absurd by a witty comparison with the ideal, or at least the preferred
simile	when one thing is compared directly to another thing, using the words 'like' or 'as'
symbolism	when an object, a person or a thing is used to represent another thing
theme	a central idea examined by an author

Checkpoint answers

CHECKPOINT 1   It allows the reader to be presented with background information on the Ewells' poverty, lack of personal pride and their status within the community.

CHECKPOINT 2   In contrast to Atticus, who treats his children as individuals (see Chapter 1), Miss Caroline's educational methods appear to make no room for the individual.

CHECKPOINT 3   They are effective because they force the children to think about how they would feel if they were in Boo's position. This reminds us of when Atticus talks to Scout in Chapter 3 and tells her 'You never really understand a person until you consider things from his point of view' (p. 35).

CHECKPOINT 4   Mr Radley blocks the hole so that Boo cannot leave presents for the children any more – so that he can have no contact with the outside world.

CHECKPOINT 5   It shows that Mrs Dubose has forgiven Jem for his actions, and also signifies that she is at last at peace.

CHECKPOINT 6   The eavesdropping technique is used by the author to get information directly to the reader through Scout.

CHECKPOINT 7   Atticus says that the children made Mr Cunningham stand in Atticus's shoes for a moment.

CHECKPOINT 8   Jem's four kinds: 'There's the ordinary kind like us and the neighbours, there's the kind like the Cunninghams out in the woods, the kind like the Ewells down at the dump, and the Negroes' (Chapter 23, p. 232). Scout's one kind: 'Folks' (Chapter 23, p. 233). Consider carefully what you think – this is a tricky question, so have some clear arguments with evidence to back up your opinions.

CHECKPOINT 9   It reminds us of Mr Gilmer's comment earlier. Find this comment and compare the two. See the definition of **leitmotif**.

CHECKPOINT 10   Atticus is again trying to get the children to see things from another's point of view. You should now have a note of several times when he has asked the children to stand in a character's shoes or skin.

CHECKPOINT 11   Through the article in *The Maycomb Tribune*, Harper Lee emphasises that Tom Robinson is an innocent creature who has been harmed unnecessarily, and she repeats this **motif** as a reminder of an important **theme**. See the discussion of the mockingbird motif in **Key themes: Symbolism**.

CHECKPOINT 12   Find examples of what the judge said to Robert Ewell at the trial which might have made him feel foolish.

CHECKPOINT 13   It is Jem's arm being broken in the struggle.

CHECKPOINT 14   As Jem is an innocent harmed, and has an outward injury similar to that of Tom, he could also be linked to the mockingbird theme.

CHECKPOINT 15   Yes, several incidents have prepared us: hiding the presents, leaving Jem's trousers on the fence, putting a blanket around Scout's shoulders.

CHECKPOINT 16   They are both concerned with Maycomb County. They are both creating a pageant, with the aim of providing benefit to their community.

CHECKPOINT 17   By emotional blackmail – crying, for instance, and making them feel that they would be cowardly rather than honourable if they did nothing about what she told them.

CHECKPOINT 18   Two examples are Chapter 3 (p. 35) and Chapter 16 (p. 163). You should find several more. Compare your findings with a friend.

CHECKPOINT 19   Miss Caroline 'looked and smelled like a peppermint drop' (Chapter 2, p. 22). Mrs Dubose's mouth was 'like a clam hole at low tide' (Chapter 11, p. 113).